TESTOSTERONE REPLACEMENT THERAPY

-A Recipe for Success-

DR JOHN CRISLER

DISCLAIMER

The information contained in this publication is for educational purposes only, and is in no way a substitute for the advice of a qualified health care provider. Appropriate medical therapy, including the use of pharmaceutical compounds and Over-the-Counter (OTC) supplements, should be tailored for the individual, as no two people are alike. The author does not recommend self-medicating with any compound, as you should consult with a qualified physician who can determine your individual situation. Any use of the information presented in this publication for medical therapy is done strictly at your own risk, and no responsibility is implied or intended on the part of the author, contributors, or the publisher.

ISBN 978-0-9837739-4-8
Medicine, Health, Chemistry, Endocrinology

TABLE OF CONTENTS

ABOUT THE AUTHOR

JOHN CRISLER, DO
Founder and CMO
All Things Male Center for Men's Health
Clinical Associate Professor--Michigan State University College of Osteopathic Medicine

"Dr. John" Crisler is an Osteopathic Physician located in Lansing, Michigan. He has distinguished himself in the field of Age Management Medicine by developing new treatment protocols for hormonal evaluation and optimization which have influenced the way physicians all over the world treat their patients.

He provides special emphasis on Testosterone Replacement Therapy and the treatment of Subclinical Hypothyroidism and Adrenal Fatigue and is one of few physicians who address the dreaded Post Finasteride Syndrome (PFS). There are good reasons why individuals have traveled to be seen in his clinic from all fifty States, as well as—at last count—twenty eight foreign countries. Commanding a substantial Internet following, "Dr John" founded the first Internet Forum on TRT moderated by a physician, and has answered more medical questions pro bono than any doctor in the history of the Internet.

His ethical standards led to being featured in an article in Playboy Magazine, called "Dr T to the Rescue" ("Dr T", standing for testosterone, is Dr. John's nickname). Dr. Crisler is a mainstay at medical conferences in the age management field. He has lectured, co-hosted and moderated across the country and around the world. He enjoys training fellow physicians, as well as the public, and is known as an informative, dynamic and highly entertaining speaker.

For more information, please go to:

www.AllThingsMale.com

NOTE: An Advice-Only-Consult (AOC) is now available.

TRT A FEW WORDS OF THANKS

I am eager to acknowledge the mentors and colleagues who have not only shaped my thinking within the realms of hormonal optimization—and of life, in general--but also provide the kind of companionship exclusively limited to those who share a common passion.

To paraphrase someone much wiser than myself, any glimpses I have seen over the horizon came while I was standing upon their shoulders:

Dr. Henry Beckmeyer, Dr. Lionel Bissoon, Dr. Anna Cabecca, Dr. Jeffrey Dach, Dr. Nick Delgado, Dr. Mark Gordon, Dr. Sharon McQuillan, Dr. Frank Nordt, Dr. Sangeeta Pati, Dr. Edward Rosick, Dr. Ronald Rothenberger, Dr. Neal Rouzier, and Dr. Eugene Shippen.

I am also delighted to honor some lay persons without whom I could not get along. Thank you for the blessings you bring to my life:

My Forum Moderators, from the www.AllThingsMale.com/forum: "Wise Guy", "Bulldog", "hebsie", "BadAssBlues" and "Chilln".

Mr. Ingraban Deters, who has spent time, and material, he did not have to give in order to help me, at all points along the way.

Mr. Scott Spink, whose never-ending friendship and business expertise are more valuable, and more appreciated, than words can say.

My Internet buddies, Mr. Gene Devine and Mr. Keith Willse...I'll never understand what I did to deserve such friendship.

Mr. Nelson Vergel—a man whose professional training is as an engineer, yet has become a true leader in this field via his book and ExcelMale.com site—without whom this book likely would not be in your hands at this time. He taught me the ropes with respect to book publishing, and kept me on schedule. Thank you for freely sharing your years of experience.

FORWARD

Doctor John Crisler, author of *"TRT: A Recipe for Success"* has combined his medical experiences into a powerful path for men to follow who are seeking direction in solving their testosterone problems. There is nothing that speaks more truly than long-term clinical experience!

What became clear for me from the earliest days of testosterone treatment was the diversity of clinical presentations and responses to treatment that pointed to genetic, environmental, health habit and lifestyle differences that made each patient a unique "case of one". Testing and treatment required constant re-adjustments to arrive at good clinical results. It took years of "practicing medicine" to become skilled enough to provide quality results in most cases. This author has arrived at the door of excellence in individualized care that is required for quality results as the result of years of firsthand experience.

One can "review" the literature endlessly searching for the right answers, but each will be disappointed at the confusion found at every turn, supported by "epidemiologic" non-sense that now is pervasive in the "peer reviewed literature". One can easily find exactly opposite conclusions for almost any effect, benefit or "side effect" from treatments with testosterone. Our science is failing to direct clear, high quality answers for risks and benefits of treatment or to outline best medical practices for physicians to follow.

What epidemiology cannot do is to define the individual differences in specific endocrine aspects that every doctor sees in every patient sitting before them. Epidemiology smooths out the differences and obliterates the "outliers" who have specific genetic differences in attempts to define statistical "truths" through data manipulation designed to "ferret out" the pure effects of one aspect or another. What they end up with are studies that try to make all individuals similar within defined boundaries when, in truth, all individuals represent completely unique composites of their inherent biologic differences - Apples and Oranges! The "Normal Ranges" seen in every lab test NEVER defines the optimal level for an individual. Being "within the Normal Range" on a test does NOT make the result "Normal" for the individual.

Epidemiologists cloud rather than clarify the parameters of individualized clinical medicine.

Most physicians get little or no training in the evaluation and treatment of arguably the most common endocrinopathy in aging men, testosterone deficiency. Sadly, this is true of ALL specialties, from Family Practice and Internal Medicine to Urologists and even Endocrinologists. Most physicians rely on ever changing "Practice Guidelines", established by well meaning, "Ivory Tower" professors. But these "Guidelines" do a poor job of answering the individual patient's clinical problems. Part of the problem is that they are designed by highly educated, intelligent researchers who have ZERO or near ZERO personal experience treating men with testosterone! Then physicians, who have little or no training at all, turn to the "Guidelines" for help in managing their patients and you have "the blind leading the blind"!!! Frustration is the most common result by patients expecting to find good clinical results to their multiple physical, metabolic and sexual difficulties. The other source of the "education" that physicians receive today comes from the "Drug Reps" for topical testosterone replacement that has become a major limb of the pharmaceutical industry. They have, through advertising, established the "Low T" movement in medicine today, but there is little time spent on the diagnostic "workup" or the many things that require individualized testing for successful results.

For those men looking for testosterone treatments that will give them a diversity of options and best chance of success, *"TRT: A Recipe for Success"* will provide many clear pathways to explore. I highly recommend it!

Eugene Shippen, M. D. and author of "The Testosterone Syndrome".

Dr. Eugene Shippen. Photo courtesy of Keith Willse.

INTRODUCTION

Much has happened in the field of Testosterone Replacement Therapy (TRT) medicine since the first version of this paper in 2004, with subsequent revision in 2010. We are getting better and better at diagnosing the insidious condition known as hypogonadism (low testosterone, or "Low T"), and at administering appropriate medical therapy. But we still have a long way to go. In fact-- and surprisingly--at this point in time, gentlemen who  frequent Internet message boards tend to know much more about TRT than do their own doctors!

The dangers of ignoring the hypogonadal state — and even the low normal testosterone level state--have been well established. Study after study ring true for what we intuitively knew all along: a man's body runs on testosterone. The testosterone depleted body is less able to regulate, and therefore protect, itself. The subsequent toll on health, and happiness, extends across the human race. It affects the man; it affects the man's loved ones. Simply, when there's not much testosterone in the body, there isn't much gas in the tank.

Of special import, with respect to overcoming the resistance of a medical community mired in an age old fallacy which was never properly proven to begin with—that TRT increases the risk of prostate cancer--is the irrefutable proof we now possess it clearly does not. But old, well-entrenched ideas are not easily abandoned; no matter how many thousands of men swear TRT restored their lives.

Physicians who stay current--and have remained men and women of science--now see the absolute requirement for proper treatment of this, the most under-diagnosed, and under-treated, malady in America today. Validation comes from the major pharmaceutical companies, who are, as a group, jumping on the bandwagon to introduce their respective versions of testosterone delivery systems.

You won't find many scientific studies in this book. Dr. Eugene Shippen's excellent Foreword describes why: the single-minded pursuit by Epidemiologists to determine a one-size-fits-all protocol, descriptive and effective for every adult male, completely ignores the unavoidable fact we simply are not all alike. An excellent example is the highly flawed concept, in practical (mis)use, of "normal range". The infinite hormonal diversity across the population means we must tailor each patient's evaluation, and subsequent regimen; not just upon initial presentation, but in long-term follow-up as well. The attempt by statistical evaluation to compress all men into a monolithic "standard patient" also ignores the fact successful treatment requires the practitioner to adjust medications, and dosages, until the individual "sweet spots" are found; not just for a given patient, but literally for each hormone. Doing otherwise is as futile as trying to hit a moving target with a gun that insists upon rigid placement.

Dr. Shippen also points out what happens when the researchers themselves know almost nothing about the subject they are investigating. The vast majority of "scientific studies" in this field of medicine are so poorly designed, executed, and evaluated they bear little resemblance to the realities of the human hormonal milieu. That is why they all too often extrapolate to completely unwarranted conclusions; and are stunningly contrary to the practical experience of those well-practiced in the art.

Their failures are also compounded by the issue of bias. Or is it coincidence any "scientific study" critical of TRT always gets front page billing—within the scientific journal community, and mass media--while simultaneously ignoring the multitudes of studies already in existence profoundly to the contrary?

So, while many studies are indeed useful for proving mechanism (the various receptor actions, hormonal interactions, and pathways, for instance), the above shortcomings mean they are not very useful for telling us what to actually do with our patients. They do not provide a practical recipe, if you will, for directing care. This book is meant to give a good start. Success will take constant practice, over time, as experience in getting to know hormonal manipulation is no different than any other area of medical care. Knowing the science is foundational, of course, but reading a cook book has never turned anyone into a French chef.

Those who can only parrot the dismissive drumbeat "show me a study", while attempting to discredit the successful work of others—those who are actually getting good results with their patients, and solving the tough cases--are really saying "I do not understand hormones". For if they did, I believe, they would come to see how intuitive—I'd say *Osteopathic*—this all becomes...once one is used to standing upon the slippery rocks of constantly changing hormone levels, genetic variation, environmental effects, and the other various and sundry influencing factors so numerous we may never complete the list. The most successful physicians in our field — the ones who have transcended from medical practitioner into true *healers* — all know these things.

Once the hearts and minds war is won for a given physician with respect to recognizing the need to correct the hypogonadal state, by providing TRT, he or she still must learn — as with all medical therapies — exactly how to do so. And given the time constraints presented by today's challenges to implementing new medical therapies--while simultaneously battling their segments of the regulatory and business worlds — who has an extra week to set aside, to learn all this? The sad truth is, at this point in time, lay persons must familiarize themselves with respect to TRT, in order to find physicians competent in this field, make successful argument/demand for appropriate care, and get the TRT they deserve. There is no better example in today's medical world of patients needing to take charge of their own health. This book was written for them.

From what I hear, many a man has printed the earlier versions of my original two papers, so he could personally hand it to his own physician. It is meant as a stand-alone document, to include all the essentials a medical practitioner needs to know in order to diagnose, test, and treat Low T. Consider this to be a practical "Recipe for Success" for TRT, if you will.

If you are a man suffering the symptoms of Low T, buy this book. If you are a doctor who has been given this book by a patient, please read it. Your patients--and their partners---will love you for it.

– CHAPTER ONE –

A Few Words About The Decision To Start TRT

All options should be explored, to find the cause of the Low T, prior to initiating this kind of treatment. We don't "do" TRT just to "do" TRT. The goal of this therapy is health and happiness, not performance enhancement. And we don't chase numbers on a laboratory printout; meaning men who are not suffering the symptoms of Low T do not get TRT just because they think they want to be at the top of "normal range" on some laboratory printout. The same people who state we should not chase numbers while considering testosterone levels at the bottom of the range need to be just as respectful of the concept as we approach the top.

On proper evaluation, sometimes we can alleviate the stressor which is causing the problem, and so right the hypogonadal state. This would always be vastly preferable to placing a(nother) drug in your body. Because in this case, you are not just taking a new medication; you are, literally, seizing control of an endocrine system. Supplementing testosterone causes the body to shut down its own production in response. The factory production line for testosterone may not be producing very well, but at least it is still running. Disrupting the body's mechanisms — sometimes permanently — brings with it responsibilities beyond which we have yet to fully comprehend. So this decision is not to be made lightly.

Even though the health dangers of ignoring the hypogonadal ("low testosterone") state are well established, you have to know there are also risks to TRT. If the blood is not properly monitored, you run an increased chance of Polycythemia ("thick blood"), because testosterone stimulates erythrocytosis (production of red blood cells); or exposing a previously undetected coagulability (blood clotting) disorder, which can cause a serious cardiovascular event. If estrogen is not properly managed, when necessary, it can cause gynecomastia (male breast growth), high blood pressure, depression, sexual dysfunction, and maybe even some forms of cancer.

At the very least, no man enjoys the sight, and feel, of his testicles atrophying (shrinking). They are no longer being used by the body, to produce testosterone; a natural response to the hormonal supplementation. Sperm production decreases as well, though TRT is not birth control. Of note, this is also a great reason to always add in regular HCG shots to every TRT protocol. More on that later.

As under-dosing brings no relief, and may even make things worse, over-dosing the testosterone also brings its own risks. At this point I would be remiss were I to fail to recognize the common misconception among human adult males, somehow ingrained into our collective psyche, which convinces us "If some is good, more is better!" With respect to testosterone supplementation, this clearly is not the case.

It's pretty obvious from the above examples that TRT must be properly managed, and if it is not being administered by a physician who is knowledgeable in the field, these risks can be very serious....just like for every other medical therapy in existence. The true experts in our field know good and well physician lack of expertise leads to bad results.

And that only poorly designed, conducted and evaluated scientific studies, improperly extrapolated to a completely unwarranted conclusion, show TRT is inherently dangerous.

Fortunately, studies have shown withdrawing the TRT usually allows the body to return to its previous state. Unfortunately, that usually means returning to the fatigue, brain fog, depression and sexual dysfunction which originally brought the patient in to seek treatment.

– CHAPTER TWO –

Testosterone And Its Production/ The Two Basic Varieties Of Low T

Below is a diagram of what is called the HPTA (Hypothalamus-Pituitary-Testicular-Axis). It is the production line, if you will, which delivers testosterone to the bloodstream:

The HPT Axis

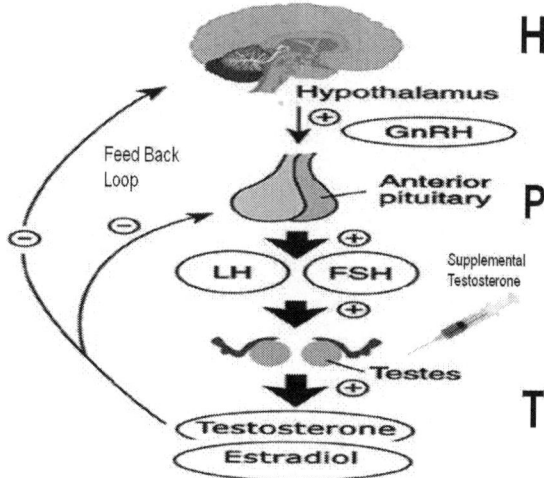

We are only now beginning to learn the various influences which affect the first component of the process, the hypothalamus. Just remember, the things which are bad for you, are bad for the stimulation of the hypothalamus. And therefore it just never gets started right on the testosterone production line.

The hypothalamus is responsible, as far as testosterone production is concerned, for producing a hormone called GnRH (Gonadotropin Releasing Hormone), which then travels by a special dedicated, or "portal", circulatory system to the pituitary gland, the "master gland" of the body. The pituitary then produces—along with a host of other important hormones, also individually regulated—two hormones, known collectively as the gonadotropins. They are Luteinizing Hormone (LH), and Follicle Stimulating Hormone (FSH).

LH is most responsible for stimulating what are called the Leydig Cells within the testicles to produce testosterone. FSH works more on the Sertoli Cells, which make sperm for reproductive purposes.

Primary Hypogonadism refers to testicular failure, to whatever extent. The causes of testicular failure are many: infection (such as mumps orchitis; when the mumps "goes down"); undescended testes (which is why they try to correct a "cryptic testicle" surgically, as soon as necessary); radiation (from nuclear disaster, or XRAY therapy—why they cover you down there with a sheet of lead); surgery (some men who have vasectomies lose ground with respect to testosterone levels); genetic and developmental disorders (such as Klinefelters Syndrome, where two X—female—chromosomes combine with the male Y chromosome, producing a XXY situation, instead of XY); liver and kidney disease; hemochromatosis (iron storage disease where the metal accumulates in the body; treatment is simply having regular blood draws, known as therapeutic phlebotomies); injury (YIKES! That is all we can say about that one); cancer treatment (chemotherapy and/or radiation can lower testosterone; temporarily or permanently); testicular cancer; testicular torsion (twisting of the gland on its stalk, a surgical emergency); and other chronic diseases (such as Rheumatoid Arthritis).

I would be remiss to fail to remind all men to examine their testicles on a regular basis. Once a month — such as on the first of each month, in the shower, while they are all soapy and slippery — just like for women to self-examine their breasts. You might consider this a "couple's exercise" even. Testicular cancer is the number one cancer killer of younger men. Feel for any kind of lump. IF you find one, call your doctor IMMEDIATELY.

With Primary Hypogonadism, the LH levels will tend to be high, because it is the testicles which are failing. So the pituitary gland attempts to drive them harder. You have high LH, but still end up with Low T.

Hypogonadotropic (secondary) Hypogonadism is when the pituitary gland does not produce enough LH to adequately stimulate the testicles. So both LH and T are low. This is the more common condition amongst men, because so many more negative influences can cause the Hypothalamus-Pituitary complex to not work right:

MANY medications (the list seems endless: chronic pain control, corticosteroid therapy, antidepressants); hemochromatosis (again); all manner of nutritional deficiencies; radiation; rapid; significant weight loss; anabolic steroid, or even prohormone use (temporary or permanent);

surgery; trauma (the pituitary gland does not like being knocked around); tumors (such as those producing the hormone prolactin); genetic problems (such as Kallman's Syndrome, which also can cause the inability to smell, known as "anosmia"); certain inflammatory diseases; HIV/AIDS; obesity; even diabetes. Here are some examples:

- Opioids
- Corticosteroids
- Antidepressants
- Cimetidine
- Chemotherapy

- Radiation
- Spironolactone
- Ketoconazole
- Statins

"Normal aging" is also usually listed as a cause of Secondary Hypogonadism. We refuse to accept it is "normal" to get sick, weak, depressed, and impotent. The association between Low T and cardiovascular disease, diabetes, depression, dementia and sexual function is very strong, as is the ability of TRT to lesson, even completely resolve, these issues. While proving that TRT prolongs lifespan is tricky scientifically, it is abundantly clear from the reports of our patients it vastly improves what is coming to be known as "Health span".

– CHAPTER THREE –

SCREENING FOR HYPOGONADISM

Should every adult male patient who presents at the doctor's office be automatically screened for hypogonadism? Given, it sure would be nice to have a permanent record of the baseline testosterone level while he is young, fit and strong. We could then know his particular "sweet spot". That would certainly help direct medical decision making later on, if and when any symptoms consistent with Low T appear.

In fact, about half of all men over the age of fifty are hypogonadal, and many more who are even younger; some, much younger. Certainly their answers on the Medical History form will lead the way toward suspicion of Low T, but subjective (patient reported) complaints related to this insidious condition are "sensitive" (reliably discover) without being very "specific" (pointing to a particular medical issue). Clinical suspicion is further clouded by the fact there is no way to correlate either the number of individual complaints, or the relative magnitude of each, to the severity of the hypogonadotropic state, once you get laboratory testing.

Additionally, the foibles of laboratory analysis--either due to the daily variability in hormone levels, or inaccuracy unavoidably inherent in laboratory testing methodology and interpretation—renders evaluation of the hormonal state, at times, much more an art than a science. We will explore the true nature of hormonal testing, and especially the concept of the "normal range", a bit later. Diagnosing--and treating--a hormonal issue get tricky. While lecturing on this, and other subjects of Interventional Endocrinology (a phrase I love, created by my pal Dr. Mark Gordon), I tell the physicians in attendance, with respect to evaluating hormones through lab work, the results are but one piece of the puzzle. In fact, they must learn to become quite comfortable with feeling like they are constantly walking upon slippery rocks.

The number one complaint which should hoist the proverbial red flag that Low T is present is Erectile Dysfunction (ED). But Lack of Libido (sexual desire) is superior in both sensitivity and specificity. Astute practitioners appreciate we must distinguish between a lack of desire, and the ability to perform. Clearly, wanting to, and being able to, are two different things; but are intimately intertwined, of course.

Lack of Libido is also the symptom of hypogonadism which, aside from all the seriously deleterious effects of Low T (cardiovascular disease, diabetes, osteoporosis, depression, dementia, etc.), is most likely to bring the patient to actively seek TRT—and to remain compliant in the subsequent treatment regimen. As I told writer Pat Jordan, for his excellent article titled after my nickname in the field, in Playboy Magazine, "Dr. T to the Rescue" (April 2007) "As long as you treat his sexual dysfunction, a man won't mind you also made him healthier".

– CHAPTER FOUR –

Initial and Follow-Up Labs

Following the taking of a good Medical History — as having the symptoms of Low T *can* be as diagnostic as basic laboratory analysis, in some cases (more on that later)--which tests should be run as part of your initial hypogonadism workup?

Following is my list, but certainly other specialists in this area of medicine run expanded or attenuated panels, per individual clinical experience, expertise and case complexity. Of note, additional tests which should be included to complete the true comprehensive Age Management Medicine workup (i.e. inflammatory markers, fasting insulin, comprehensive thyroid study, etc.) have been omitted; this paper is concerned solely with the administration of TRT.

Some of the below tests you could run, in order to round-out the hormonal picture. Please look to their respective individual descriptions to follow. Here they are:

- Testosterone, Total
- Testosterone, Bioavailable
- Testosterone, Free
- SHBG
- LH
- FSH
- DHT
- DHEA-S
- Estradiol ("sensitive" assay only)
- Chemistries
- CBC
- PSA
- Prolactin (if T <150, or if sexual dysfunction even after proper TRT)

If you have a family history of an inherited blood clotting disorder then consider these labs as well. Your doctor will know what to do with them:

- PT
- APTT
- Factor V Leiden mutation
- Factor VIII
- Factor XI

Below is a list of the hormone tests, from the major laboratory chains, using the acceptable LC/MS technology:

Quest Diagnostics
Testosterone, Total #15983
Testosterone, Free and Total #36170
Testosterone, Free, Bioavailable, and Total #14966

Estradiol, Ultrasensitive #30289
Estrone LC/MS #23244

LabCorp
Testosterone Total #070001

Testosterone, Bioavailable w/SHBG #500650

Estradiol #500108
Estrone #500634
DHEA-S #500161

[NOTE: the "Sensitive Estradiol" #140244 uses immunoassay, but is somewhat acceptable when cost is an issue).

FOLLOW-UP LABS

These can be run as early as three weeks after initiating, or changing the dose, for TD's (transdermals, "through the skin", testosterone gel). Four weeks for one-shot-per-week (initial) testosterone injection protocols. The time delay provides for stabilization of the HPTA (which will decrease your own production of testosterone, in response to the TRT), Sex Hormone Binding Globulin (SHBG) adjustment, and the pharmacodynamics (what the hormone does in the body) of the testosterone delivery system. It takes time for the body to adjust. Adding, or changing the dose, of a medication is likened to dropping a pebble into a pond.

- Total Testosterone
- Bioavailable Testosterone (AKA "Free and Loosely Bound")
- Free Testosterone
- Estradiol (specify "sensitive" assay for males)
- DHEA-S
- CBC
- Comprehensive Metabolic Panel
- LH (if you want to know if the system is suppressed, or if a transdermal gel is getting in)
- FSH (same as above)

– CHAPTER FIVE –

Individual Laboratory Tests Explained

SEX HORMONE BINDING GLOBULIN

Why am I starting off the individual lab test descriptions with Sex Hormone Binding Globulin (SHBG)? Because it is the centerpiece of every proper hormonal evaluation; without knowing its level, you cannot know how much of any sex hormone is actually available for the body to use. Omitting SHBG from your testing turns a good medical work-up into a mere guessing game.

It is also one of the topics I spend the most time thinking about.

SHBG is produced mainly by the liver, and then released into the bloodstream. It strongly binds to almost all the sex hormones it finds floating around there, both "male" and "female" varieties. These are all found in both genders, by the way, and have powerful effects in each. Once they are tightly bound to SHBG, they are, from a practical standpoint, unavailable for us to use because they may not also then bind to their respective hormone receptor. Only hormones which float freely in the region around the receptors can bind to them, and therefore initiate whatever effects that hormone eventually brings. The old analogy is the hormone is like the key, with the receptor being its respective lock.

We are learning some surprising things about hormones, binding proteins, and receptor actions; but this explanation shall have to suffice for the time being.

But basically, the lower the SHBG level, the greater the amount of testosterone available for us to use. The higher the SHBG, less testosterone—of the Total Testosterone--is "bioavailable". When asked, between the two, whether I prefer SHBG to be high or low, I choose high. Surprised?

First, I must be clear that I am now referring to the patient who is about to start, or is already on, TRT. Because prior to that, higher SHBG means the gentleman must make more testosterone to have enough left over that is still free, and therefore useful. As a man ages--and his ability to produce testosterone decreases--this begins to have a real effect. Now add in the fact we tend to make more SHBG with age.

Certainly, having more Free Testosterone is a good thing...but we have to remember the same thing happens to the other sex hormones as well, like estrogen. If SHBG is higher, I can always add in more testosterone, to mass action over the top of it. But there are gentlemen with low SHBG, so often very little estrogen is tolerated, due to the fact so much of it is left free, to feminize.

Amongst a few of the sex hormones, here is the order of strength of binding to SHBG:

DHT > Testosterone > Androstenediol > Estradiol (E2) > Estrone (E1)

So you can see, by the above, the stronger the androgenicity ("maleness") of the hormone, the stronger SHBG latches onto it. That means if testosterone and estrogen levels are equal, more — and *more*--estrogen is left free to affect you.

We do see evidence of a variability in the "stickiness" of SHBG. We will be publishing more on that topic in the future.

SHBG level is manipulated by many simultaneous factors; with the end result the summation of the influences of the whole. It increases with estrogen, and sometimes, with thyroid replacement therapy (even small dosages). Factors which lower SHBG are high levels of insulin (as in Type II diabetes), growth hormone, IGF-1, prolactin, transcortin (a circulating protein that loosely binds to, and so carries glucocorticoids, like cortisol--the "stress hormone"; it also carries progesterone, another important hormone), and, generally, androgens.

Please note that means TRT itself can lower SHBG, and so make more free testosterone. This is a double benefit--unless bioavailable estrogen then gets out-of-control.

Generally, I do not attempt to manipulate SHBG. I treat it like a cork bobbing on the water, and work around it, as it comes. But I have in rare cases sought to lower it. You can do so by taking 50mg of Danazol orally per day. There is nothing you can do to elevate SHBG in any practical healthy manner.

To make sure you grasp the interactions, Type II diabetes means high insulin, which drives SHBG down. The body recognizes the resultant higher free testosterone, and subsequently lowers testosterone production. You end up with Low T. Even though maintaining the same Free

33

Testosterone level is important, it is clear to us that the Total Testosterone level still has significant value. Also, diabetes on its own lowers testosterone levels. This serves as a good exercise to understand the relationships between these factors.

We will discuss the hormones individually over the coming pages. Just so you know, DHEA in free form is only weakly bound to SHBG. DHEA-S, the sulfated "S" form, is mostly what comes out of the liver. Androstenedione, the hormone we can't get any longer (thanks to former baseball player Mark McGuire's little cover up), is a weak androgen that does not bind to SHBG..

I would be remiss not to add that in my experience, low SHBG is strongly associated with anxiety. More on that in a later release.

TOTAL TESTOSTERONE

This is the laboratory test your doctor will most likely focus on if he or she is not well-practiced in the art, for it is more likely to be used to *deny* the man the TRT he wants—and deserves. Total Testosterone simply tells the concentration of testosterone in the bloodstream, but only at the particular time the blood sample was drawn. We must always keep this in mind: it's just a "snapshot" of a rapidly changing hormonal environment.

This is because the level of testosterone in the bloodstream changes throughout the day. In fact, the more it changes, the better it is for you, as young men have more variability in their serum T levels than do older men—even in situations where each may reach the same peaks, and troughs. It would appear entropy (randomness) is part, and parcel, of youth.

Since a single blood draw is only a "snap shot" at that particular time, we never know if we happened to hit the peak, the trough, or somewhere in between. That is why we strive to treat actual patients, by their symptoms; we are treating a living, breathing human being...not merely treating ink on a piece of laboratory printout paper. The best physicians, the ones who have become true "healers", look at it this way.

Of note, this is why a 24 hour urine collection is the best way to tell how much testosterone a man produces throughout the entire day, or how much of a T gel is being absorbed, as a fairly reliable fraction (variations in this proportion will be explored in future publishing) is excreted into the urine. Scientists call this getting the "Area Under the Curve" (AUC), and it removes the rollercoaster-like drawback of a single blood draw.

Of note, I do not like spot urine panels. They are not much better than a "spot" blood draw.

The effects of Sex Hormone Binding Globulin (SHBG), in tightly binding the testosterone in the bloodstream, and thereby making it unavailable for use, makes this test much less than optimal. But Total Testosterone is always important for titration (adjustment) of dosing; as long as we keep in mind the shortcomings of this basic assay.

Many physicians will deny patients TRT when Total T is at low-normal levels; even when the poor man has all the symptoms of Low T. This demonstrates a basic lack of understanding of how sex hormones, and laboratory testing, work. More on the hot topic of "normal range" later.

If Total Testosterone comes back at less than 150, something is very wrong; that's just way too low. The patient should be sent for an MRI of the pituitary, in case the issue is a pituitary adenoma. You should also then automatically run a prolactin test.

BIOAVAILABLE TESTOSTERONE

This is where we get the "bang" for the hormonal buck, so to speak. This is the actual amount of testosterone the body has available for use; specifically, the concentration of hormone available in the space around the androgen receptor, to bind to it, and therefore initiate the effects of the hormone.

Bioavailable testosterone (Bio-T) equals the sum of the Free Testosterone, plus that which is loosely bound to other carrier proteins in the blood, primarily albumin. Albumin, which is made by the liver, is much like egg white. Testosterone can easily separate from these loosely binding carrier proteins, and so becomes of use to us, or "bioavailable". That is why the Bio-T assay is also known as "Free and Loosely Bound" at some labs.

These loosely binding carrier proteins contrast Sex Hormone Binding Globulin (SHBG), which very tightly binds androgens, rendering them unavailable for binding to the androgen receptor. *For a given amount* of testosterone produced, higher SHBG means less Bioavailable Testosterone. The reverse is also true.

So Bioavailable Testosterone is the gold standard for serum testosterone evaluation, and *usually* comprises only about half of the Total Testosterone.

FREE TESTOSTERONE

Since testosterone does not dissolve very well into the blood, only a very small amount floats around "freely", about 1-2% of the Total Testosterone.

If Bio-T is not readily available, Free T may be a second choice substitute, as Bio-T and Free T serum concentrations are usually well correlated. Still, better than Total Testosterone, though, when comparing lab values to clinical response.

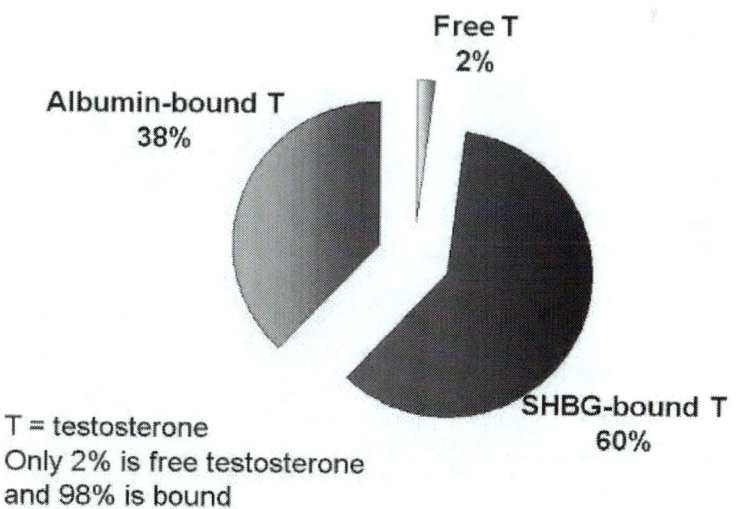

Testosterone Fractions in the Blood

Free T 2%

Albumin-bound T 38%

SHBG-bound T 60%

T = testosterone
Only 2% is free testosterone
and 98% is bound

DHT

DHT is made from Testosterone, by the 5-alpha reductase enzyme. It is several times more androgenic than its parent molecule, and the rate of this conversion varies greatly across the male population.

It is associated with everything from male aggression, to prostate growth, to hair loss. But it also plays a very important role in producing libido, or sexual desire. I'll explain why later, but this is why transdermal T gels are typically the best at restoring sexual function.

This assay *may* be of value to draw, up-front and at follow-up, especially if a transdermal testosterone delivery system is preferred by the patient. But we have now come to appreciate that it is more likely the amount of DHT produced by direct conversion from testosterone *inside* the cells which best describe the patient's symptoms, and the evaluation of certain other metabolic by-products gives us a better understanding of how much of that conversion is actually happening. That discussion is beyond the scope of this basic paper; I'll make sure to cover it in a future update.

I do not consider DHT an "evil hormone". In my professional opinion, medications which block the 5-AR enzyme, such as the prescription drugs used to combat hair loss, are to be avoided; especially in light of the emergence of the dreaded Post Finasteride Syndrome (PFS). We will discuss that topic, too, in future updates.

If you are experiencing issues with hair loss, with or without TRT, I recommend using a topical application, to directly affect the hair at its root.

ESTRADIOL

Why is it important to follow a "female sex hormone" in adult males? Because estrogen is in men, as well as women. And for both it has benefits, and deleterious effects, depending on its concentration, and balance.

You don't have to have so much of it you cry while watching the movie "Gladiator" (according to one of my patients), watch Oprah, subscribe to Redbook Magazine, and grow a pair of breasts your girlfriend would be jealous of, to be suffering estrogen problems. In fact, we have found modulating mere imbalances in estrogen—and usually with OTC supplements--can have profound effects on health and happiness.

On the other hand, I do not treat high estrogen in absence of symptoms. I want to be clear about that.

Estradiol (E2) is considered the major form of estrogen in the body. It is quite proliferative of the tissues, especially the prostate gland. That is why it is the one we follow the most. There are two other major forms of estrogen, estrone (E1) and estriol (E3), but (E2) is the player of choice. Together, they add up to Total Estrogens.

So "estrogen" is actually a class of hormones. That means the opposite of "estrogen" is not "testosterone"…it is "androgen"; testosterone is but one hormone in that group. Now you know.

While E2 is the major "female sex hormone" of interest in foundational TRT, estrone (E1) also can play an influential role. A fascinating topic, but we must leave a detailed discussion to future publishings. Basically, evaluation of the other members of the hormonal class "estrogen" (E1, E3, as well as other estrogen metabolites), via serum or even a 24 hour urine panel, may help explain gynocomastia, and other elevated estrogen symptoms, predict cancer risk, demonstrate the body's ability to detoxify itself, sexual function, etc.

There are several reasons why estrogen status is so important to assess. It should not be ignored in any proper hypogonadism work-up (and subsequent TRT regimen). First, you need to draw a baseline level, so you know about how much estrogen the gentleman is naturally producing, and also to compare to the testosterone level. There are rare cases where testosterone is adequate, yet estrogen elevated, or merely disproportionate. Elevated estrogen (in absolute value or proportion) can, in and of itself, explain hypogonadal symptomology.

If estrogen is elevated, controlling serum concentrations (usually with an aromatase inhibitor, which prevents the conversion of T into E; as well as the withdrawal of estrogen mimics, such as soy or flax seed) may--in very rare cases--suffice in clearing the symptoms of hypogonadism. So can detoxing the liver—another fascinating subject beyond the scope of this book--so that estrogens are properly broken down, and then expelled.

Checking estradiol after beginning the initial dose of testosterone will give the astute physician valuable information as to how the patient's individual hormonal system functions, as well as making sure estrogen does not elevate inappropriately after testosterone supplementation. The added testosterone partly converts into estrogen, and by the same enzyme, aromatase.

This is VERY important: unless you specify a "sensitive" (or "ultrasensitive", or "enhanced") assay for your male patients, the lab will default to the standard estradiol test, which is designed for women. The standard laboratory methodology is invalid for adult males. In fact, if you do that. by what is called immunoassay technique with Quest Diagnostics, a paragraph will appear below the results, directing you to run the correct test next time.

The reason for this discrepancy is the bottom of "normal range" for a woman is the top of "normal range" for a man. Here's one way of looking at it: without getting too technical, laboratory science is based on what is called the bell curve, which uses statistical analysis of a given patient population to figure out what "normal" is. Specifically, it is meant to cover 95% of the population. Aside from the issues with the concept of "normal" range (explored more fully elsewhere in this paper) the bell curve, for this test, sits well within the "normal" range for females. Therefore the hormonal concentration range appropriate to adult males falls on a very flat slope, out on the edge of the bell curve. You want your result to land on a steep slope--positive or negative--of the bell curve. Laboratory testing is best when small changes in concentrations result in large changes in the reported result.

What this all means is, simply, hormonal concentrations are too small to be reliably measured by immunoassay techniques. The laboratory methodology of choice is Liquid Chromatography/Mass Spectroscopy (LC/MS). Immunoassay technology (what they usually use) is not sufficient, as it is simply unreliable at such low hormonal concentrations. This is particularly true for estrogens in men.

I have run the standard assay, and the sensitive assay, concurrently on a number of my patients, and the two results may be as night and day. However, patient symptomology is best described by the sensitive assay. The standard assay tends to greatly overestimate estrogen. This is not only confusing but it may also lead (for undertrained physicians who treat numbers, in absence of symptoms) to the inappropriate addition of an estrogen controlling drug. Thus estrogen is inappropriately lowered, too far. And that is very bad for your health.

Estrogen is absolutely necessary for our physical health, so it must never be lowered too much. Of note, it provides the emotional component of a man's sexual being as well. Therefore, he can suffer Lack of Libido from an estrogen which is either too high, or too low. This is why estrogens must be evaluated and, when necessary, controlled properly.

The "sweet spot" estrogen concentration depends upon SHBG, as with all the sex hormones. A very general Rule of Thumb is mid-range for both. I remember it like what I enjoy in my morning coffee: Half and Half.

Some believe it is only the T/E ratio which is significant, and therefore, as long as E only "appropriately" rises with elevations in T, all is well. This is incorrect, as the absolute concentration of estrogen (actually, all of them) is of concern, too. Now especially so in light of data pointing to elevated estrogen as cause, or adjunctively encouraging, several serious disease processes; including numerous cancers, as well as significant potential for induction of sexual dysfunction (no matter the accompanying androgen load). Therefore T/E ratio is only useful for describing the cause of the symptoms, and is not to be used as a treatment goal.

LH

Luteinizing Hormone (LH), known as a gonadotropin ("gonad stimulating"), is produced by the pituitary gland, and then travels through the bloodstream down to the testicles, where it stimulates the Leydig cells found there to produce testosterone. When LH levels are high, more testosterone is produced, and when it is low, less. LH pulses throughout the 24 hour day; in fact, even the way the LH pulses has a big effect on testosterone production.

A caveat, however: LH has a short half-life (how long it takes for half of whatever is left of it to break down in the bloodstream, over and over again, until none is left) of only about 20 minutes. When you combine this fact with the pulsatile nature of its pituitary release, care must be taken to avoid placing too much weight upon the results of a single blood draw. Therefore a single LH assay serves only as a proven *example* of just how much LH the pituitary *can* produce, *at that particular moment*; not how much it is making all the time.

The most important reason to assay the gonadotrophins is to differentiate between primary and secondary (hypogonadotropic) hypogonadism. This is especially true when a HPTA-stimulating TRT protocol is attempted, with a drug of the SERM class, like clomiphene (more on that later in this paper). Or to "restart" the system, like we do after anabolic steroid (including prohormone) use, as well as other HPTA-disrupting factors. We will have to wait for a future update to talk about all that.

Dramatically lowered LH can indicate a transdermal testosterone preparation is indeed penetrating. This can be quite valuable information in confusing cases, especially when the preferred 24 hour urine panel (best when assessing TRT using T gels) is not available. Please refer to the section on T gels. Other than that, there is no point in running the LH test once TRT is established; it is expected to be, and will remain, suppressed, as long as the TRT is on board.

FSH

The second of the gonadotropin hormones is Follicle Stimulating Hormone (FSH), produced by the pituitary gland.

The 3-4 hour long half-life, and less pulsatile production, of Follicle Stimulating Hormone (FSH) can actually make it a better marker, *in some cases*, for gonadotropin production, when evaluating HPTA activity. It is less an acute phase reactant (a cool sounding phrase we like to use, that simply refers to something whose production is changed quickly in response to some stimulus) to varying serum androgen--and estrogen--levels than LH. Estrogen plays an important role in its suppression, so that plays in as well, and that increases its value as a marker, or indicator, of HPTA status.

FSH also provides valuable information for those patients undergoing TRT who are interested in the state of their fertility. Of note, while there are never guarantees where fertility medicine is concerned—men who rely upon TRT as birth control are known as "fathers"—in most cases, when my protocols are followed, appropriate TRT will not make a fertile man infertile. Specifically, the addition of regular HCG injections *usually* helps.

DHEA

If you perform an Internet search of "DHEA", you will learn of its many benefits. It is important for cognitive function, immune function, and cardiovascular health (the only real receptors we have found for DHEA line the cardiovascular system). Of special note, it is also strongly associated with sexual function. I have had patients report it restored their libido (even while on TRT) when they added in some DHEA (as long as you don't take too much).

It's interesting that too much DHEA in men converts to estrogen; but too much in a woman converts to testosterone.

I always monitor DHEA, and add it in where necessary. For serum testing, DHEA-S is the laboratory test of choice, not DHEA. There is so much more DHEA-S in the body than DHEA, so the test is just more accurate (more to measure). Adding to this point is the fact DHEA is weakly bound to SHBG, while DHEA-S is weakly bound to albumin. Finally, the "-S" separates from the DHEA in most tissues, so this test does better tell us how much we actually have to use.

The best way to take DHEA is in a transdermal gel. Have the compounding pharmacy mix it in the same base as your T gel, if you are on one. That way you can apply one on top of the other.

Transdermal gels (and I use gels, not creams, when possible) are more slowly released into the system, and as the "free" form (the "-S" is not added until it passes through the liver, as do pills, along with everything you eat). Adult males can start with 50mg applied to the skin (1mL of 5%, or 0.5mL of 10% gel), and, depending on their absorption, increase from there.

Second choice would be a troche (soft tablet that is placed under the tongue to dissolve), because while most of it disappears down the gullet, some of it is absorbed directly into the bloodstream through the capillaries near the surface under the tongue (like nitroglycerine tablets do, in a jiffy, for those with heart problems). Usually 25mg is about as much as you can take at a time, or it will convert to more estrogen. And you do need to take it twice per day, since it has a short half-life.

I hasten to add, any sublingual ("under the tongue") form of DHEA must be heavily flavored. It tastes terrible. In my opinion, only mint, or perhaps cinnamon, is palatable.

Last, but still well worthwhile, and is the least expensive — is the capsular form. Again, about 25mg at a time is the upper limit (some can take 50mg), and twice per day, to give more even availability, without undue conversion to estrogen.

It is important to remember to never take oral DHEA when doing any kind of urinary hormonal testing. It floods the test sample with DHEA, and its metabolites, and therefore completely throws off the results.

PROLACTIN

Prolactin is produced in males, as well as females; where it induces milk production during lactation — in both sexes if it rises enough. This is why it is tested in men who produce fluid from their nipples.

When prolactin is too high, it also causes hypogonadism, due to its effect on inhibiting the release of Luteinizing Hormone Releasing Hormone (LHRH) from the hypothalamus (the second step in the production of testosterone by the HPTA). But only about 5% of Low T cases are the result of elevated prolactin, called hyperprolactinemia. That is why we only check it under certain conditions. IF there is nipple secretion of fluid, or if Total Testosterone <150, then the test is run. If the prolactin is very high, that means a trip for an MRI of the pituitary gland. There is then a greatly increased chance of a pituitary tumor (called an adenoma, which is not a cancer) at work, making all that extra prolactin. A prolactin > 300 is pathognomotic (that means it is characteristic of a particular medical condition) for a pituitary tumor; this shows just the beginning of the wild ranges that are possible.

Because the pituitary gland sits right over where the nerves that go to the eyes cross (at the optic chiasm), a larger adenoma can affect vision, and cause headaches. Adenomas less than 10mm in size are generally just monitored (and prolactin and estrogen tightly controlled--since estrogen can make these tumors grow), and not surgically removed until they grow larger than 10mm. The procedure then is amazingly simple (easy for us to say, eh?): they go up through the nose, drill a little hole in the back, cut it out, and patch up. The patient goes home the next day.

Prolactin's serum concentration must be maintained within physiological range (meaning neither too high, nor too low). That is because it has important functions, such as maintaining immune function, as well as the LH receptors in the testicles.

And prolactin also has an important role in sexual function. My friend Dr. Eugene Shippen has shown that for men with sexual dysfunction, a 9AM FASTING draw, with a normal wake-up time, should not be above 5ng/ml. If it is, he lowers the prolactin with a dopamine agonist (a drug that acts like the hormone dopamine, and so binds to its receptors; when dopamine goes up, generally prolactin heads the other direction) like Dostinex (cabergoline), and thereby, many times, restores libido. This is why expert practitioners often test it when sexual function is still lacking, even after properly "tuning up" the patient on TRT.

Of note, Prolactin is elevated by many things, including eating and sex, so the morning draw must be done in a fasting state (no food for 12 hours). I honestly do not know how high it can go if eating while having sex.

There are also a lot of prescription medications that cause hyperprolactinemia. That is why they tend to subdue sexual function. The list is huge, but here are the some examples:

- Opioids (pain medications)
- Antidepressants
- Verapamil
- D2 antagonists
- Metoclopramide

CORTISOL

The "stress hormone". True Age Management Medicine must be well-familiarized with the ins and outs (literally) of this hormone, the only one our bodies cannot live without. Elevated levels can cause Hypogonadotropic (secondary) Hypogonadism. This is but one of the ways stress kills us.

Of note, I try controlling elevated cortisol with an OTC (Over-The-Counter) supplement called Phosphatidylserine, 300mg taken orally right before bed, with good results.

It is just as important to watch for depressed, or inappropriate, cortisol production, as well.

CBC

This is just good medicine. Ruling out anemia is important, of course, as it may actually be cause for the fatigue which brought the patient into the doctor's office.

Because testosterone stimulates the production and release of red blood cells (RBC), a process called erythrocytosis, in some cases TRT will make the blood too "thick". That condition is known as polycythemia. They must then get regular blood draws, to siphon off the excess red blood cells. Failing to heed this important point may produce serious health issues, as the patient is at increased risk for such things as a heart attack, stroke, or pulmonary embolism. It is a simple matter to run a

Complete Blood Count (CBC) each time you have labs done. Failing to do so can, sooner or later, bring disastrous results.

On the CBC, look specifically at the "H/H", (what doctors call the Hemoglobin/Hematocrit assays). Hemoglobin is the molecule that actually carries the oxygen in the blood. Hematocrit is the total percentage of the blood which is solid material. If either of the numbers 18.0/55.0, are exceeded, TRT must be withheld, to decrease the stimulation for more RBC's. But most times you can lower your numbers by simply donating blood. Of note, we are reminded that smokers, and sleep apnea sufferers, are already at increased risk for Polycythemia (and Low T).

If the 18.0/55.0 limit is exceeded, and they are deferred from a blood donation center for one reason or another, then a therapeutic phlebotomy (blood draw) is required. I see this in only a very few of my patients. I would like to add we see less of this now that we have come to appreciate testosterone shots must be delivered at an interval no greater than one week. In the old days, when doctors gave a massive injection of testosterone, say, every three weeks, they saw many more cases of Polycythemia. Smaller, more even, dosing reduces this risk substantially.

COMPREHENSIVE METABOLIC PANEL

Again, just good medicine.

Of note, many of my patients consume higher amounts of protein each day, due to muscle building interests or specialty dieting, and this is remembered when interpreting labs, because it can elevate Blood Urea Nitrogen (BUN) concentration. Nitrogen is what connects those wonderful amino acids together to make protein; they separate as they go into the bloodstream, and reconnect once again to form, for instance, muscle tissue. That is why nitrogen retention is a measure of the quality of the protein.

Also, guys who take the OTC supplement called creatine will produce elevated creatinine levels on their metabolic panel. Doctors who don't know this may think the patient is having problems with their kidneys, just as those with BUN elevations (from high protein intake) may be suspected of liver failure. Now you know better.

PSA

Prostatic Specific Antigen (PSA) is a protein that is usually inside the cells of the prostate gland. So when you find it in the bloodstream—more than just a very tiny bit of it—that means something is going on to release it from those cells. It could be physical trauma (even from a prostate exam in the doctor's office), prostate cancer, or prostatitis ("-itis" when attached to the end of a word, just means inflammation). Prostatitis can be from an infection (think of the germs that are found down in that area), or inflammation.

Worst case is an elevation in PSA is because the prostate has cancer.

Treatment for either cause of prostatitis—inflammation or infection--is the same: an antibiotic. Because the blood flow through the prostate is so poor, you have to be on them for weeks in order to get enough antibiotic into the tissue to do the job.

We follow PSA in all patients over 45, and over 40 if Family History of prostate cancer. Even with the new thoughts about the value of this test, I still like to run them. Accelerations in PSA above 0.75 per year are a contraindication (reason to abstain from treatment) to TRT, until proper follow-up by a Urologist.

You may find, at the initiation of TRT (especially in older men), when serum androgen levels are rapidly rising, PSA may, too. This is especially true when transdermal delivery systems are employed, because they more elevate DHT, and DHT causes PSA to rise (why you have to know if a patient is on a drug that lowers DHT, like the ones used for hair loss, and to shrink the prostate). Once T levels have stabilized, PSA usually drops back down to roughly baseline.

I get a PSA up front, and want them to have one every year after that. DRE (Digital Rectal Exam) is recommended once per year as well, for those above target age.

I would like to finish this section with a quick note, a peeve of mine, really, concerning the spelling of this bothersome little gland. "P-R-O-S-T-A-T-E" is the gland. "P-R-O-S-T-R-A-T-E" means lying face down.

– CHAPTER SIX –

A Few Words About What "Normal Range" Is….And Is Not

"Laboratory reference values for testosterone vary widely, and are established without clinical considerations."

Wide variability in laboratory reference values for serum testosterone.
Stephen Lazarou. Harvard Medical School, Division of Urology, Beth Israel Deaconess Medical Center, Boston, MA, USA J Sex Med 3:1085-9. 2006

How is "normal range" for hormones found? And what does "normal range" actually represent? A hormone level that is associated with health and/or happiness? Surprisingly, the answer is a resounding "No!"

In fact, "normal range" is determined purely through statistical methods. In other words, by mathematics. You should be disappointed that "normal range" is set to include ALL adult males, except the very lowest, and highest, 2.5% for a given hormone. So it covers 95% of the adult male population--no matter what state of health they are in.

That means even the ones who are sick.

Conventional medicine is therefore mired in the mistaken notion we are all alike. Please see Dr. Eugene Shippen's Foreword for much more illumination on this very important point.

Astute practitioners have come to appreciate the vast hormonal variability across the human race, and that everyone has their own respective "sweet spot" — for each hormone. They see Interventional Endocrinology (a phrase I love, created by my pal Dr. Mark Gordon) as treating real, living, breathing patients; not as if merely treating the ink on a piece of laboratory printout paper.

This misguided notion that we are all alike leads to the under-treatment, and even the refusal of treatment, for men who need, and deserve, TRT. For instance, if "normal range" is 300-1000, and an adult male patient presents with a Total Testosterone of, for instance, 325, AND the symptoms of Low T, too many physicians refuse treatment. He is, after all, "normal range". No doctor who truly understands hormones would agree.

A few words about the different "normal ranges" at different labs: From what I have read on the Internet message boards, some guys seek out laboratories for their testing where they know the top of "normal range" is higher, thinking they will then get a bigger dose of testosterone prescribed. Beside the fact more is not automatically better, we must appreciate that reference ranges are set as I already pointed out, purely through statistical means. That means each reference range is established with a given set of proprietary equipment, particular chemical reagents, and their own testing methodology.

I know this is a difficult concept to grasp, but, basically, a blood sample that produces a midrange result at one lab should also produce a midrange result at another, irrespective of different reference ranges. Think about it: the blood samples they used to statistically derive "normal range" all came from the same population.

In a reference range that goes, for example, from 250-1000, a Total Testosterone of 500 is not midrange; it is 1/3 the way up from the bottom.

If the reference range extends to 1000, that means a fair number of men will normally live at 1000. Some 2.5%, by the statistical means employed to establish "normal range", will be even higher than that. So if one of these men now presents with a Total T of 500, that means he is living with only half — perhaps less — of the testosterone his body is used to running on. IF you truly understand hormones, this is how you have to think of it.

By the way, in absence of the symptoms of Low T, I do not treat with TRT, irrespective of the laboratory results, unless they are really low (with confirmatory follow-up). There are too many variables with respect to laboratory testing. Legitimate doctors do not prescribe TRT for "performance enhancement". Very low numbers (<150ng/dL), however, must be fully worked up with a pituitary MRI, looking for the potential presence of a pituitary tumor.

That is because there are men who live very well at a Total T of only 400ng/dl. If they complain of no symptoms of Low T, I would not choose to disrupt their hormonal system by seizing control of it through TRT. It all depends on what is right for *you*. Save the TRT for later in life, when you may actually need it.

And a single test could have just happened to catch a natural low point during the day. Another very good reason why we are not chasing numbers.

You must also always take into account Sex Hormone Binding Globulin (SHBG) level, the "rollercoaster effect" mentioned previously, daily variability, and laboratory error. But the best way is to simply *talk to the patient*. As I teach my students at MSU-COM: 80% of all medical diagnosis are made purely upon Medical History (answers to basic questions about what's going on with them, and their medical past). This is very important to keep in mind in this area of medicine, because laboratory testing, and analysis, can be tricky.

– CHAPTER SEVEN –

Testosterone Delivery Systems

I want to make sure to make the point that ALL testosterone delivery systems are "bioidentical". That means the molecule is exactly the same as the one your own system makes (or used to make). In my professional opinion, improving the way the product performs in the body, for instance by the half-life of the cypionate (or enanthate) ester attached to the testosterone molecule, does not change that. The ester cleaves off over time, in pieces, and you once again have bioidentical testosterone. Without the delaying actions of the ester (a molecule consisting of chains of carbon atoms meant to increase breakdown time) you would merely have what is called a testosterone suspension, which produces a single huge spike of serum T, then quickly disappears.

Similarly, all testosterone you can take — meaning that which is not produced by your body — is "synthetic".

Now we have to decide, together with the doctor, what form of testosterone delivery system we will first try. There are two basic subsets of the major testosterone delivery systems: transdermals (TD's) and injectables (I usually use testosterone cypionate). Here are the current options:

TESTOSTERONE GELS

In my professional opinion the superior TRT modality is a transdermal (TD) delivery system. The physician and the patient should agree on this form of treatment; it is, after all, a lifestyle choice. As I have gained knowledge and experience over the years, my position now is that TD's are superior to, for instance, injectable testosterone. That is because TD's produce a serum androgen profile which varies greatly throughout the day, as it does normally in an otherwise young, strong, healthy male. It would appear that entropy (randomness) in hormone levels are part and parcel of the process of youth.

"The constant variability of serum androgens provided by T gels mimic the hormones of a young man; the stable daily level provided by T injections mimic the hormones of an old man; those of implantable pellets mimic the hormones of no man."

Other forms of TRT do not do this as well. When you seize control of the HPTA through TRT, you must consider the subsequent hormonal landscape you are creating. To my way of thinking, that means as closely following the natural pathways as possible.

TD's are easy to apply, usually well absorbed, and rapidly establish stable serum androgen levels (by the end of the third day). I recommend all practitioners first try a testosterone gel for their TRT patients. Gels are better than creams, as I want the rapid T uptake into the subdermal layer, which serves as reservoir for distribution throughout the day.

CLINICAL PEARL: Testosterone gels treat the patient; testosterone creams treat the inside of your clothing.

The reason the decision to use a transdermal T system is a lifestyle choice is because it must be allowed to dry, and to remain dry for a time, in order to allow adequate absorption. But whatever your schedule, as long as you do it that way consistently—and have testing done on the same daily regimen—it's all good.

Also, you can NEVER get T gel on a pregnant woman; you also never get it on a child, obviously. As you would expect, much is made of the risk posed by accidental transference of testosterone to others, such as children or sexual partners. Simply covering with a T-shirt has been shown to block transfer of the hormone; so application technique is important to consider in all cases.

The testosterone sinks into the skin within about an hour. One may shower, or even swim, without worry, after four hours. I remind my patients most of us have neither the time, nor the opportunity, for romance until evening, anyway (given the usual early morning application). A quick shower is always nice for a gentleman to "freshen up" prior to a romantic interlude. This simultaneously prevents accidental transfer.

TD's provide a greater boost in DHT levels, compared to injectable testosterone preparations. As DHT is responsible for all the things of manhood--literally, All Things Male--the transdermals are better at treating sexual dysfunction than are injectables. However, issues of hair loss (which I treat with a topical agent) and possible prostate morbidity (a contentiously debatable point, to be sure, but resolved in the negative, to my mind) then come into play.

This might be a good time to mention I vehemently oppose adding finasteride, or similar medication, as it will then affect the entire body:

> *"Taking a systemic DHT lowering drug to combat hair loss is like filling a tea cup in a thunderstorm."*

Transdermal T gels/creams are more likely to elevate estrogen than injections, as long as the shots are properly administered once per week. That is because aromatase, the enzyme that converts testosterone into estrogen, lives in higher concentration in the skin, along with higher concentrations of the enzyme 5-alpha-reductase, which converts testosterone into DHT. In fact, it has been shown the greater the area of application, the greater the amount of estrogen and DHT subsequently produced. This is why higher concentrations of T gel, such as 5% or 10%, which don't spread out as far, present less chance you will need to get a prescription for a drug to control estrogen.

Some have reported an increase in hair growth over the application area(s). All physicians who administer TRT must be prepared to disappoint their patients at this time by pointing out; sadly, this same effect cannot be achieved upon the scalp.

IF lifestyle allows for it, some do better by splitting the dose of the T gel, and taking half in the morning, and the rest after work. The levels are then higher than before in the evening (HINT: opportunity for romance), and also the next morning, if you train before work. This is especially true for those who have lower SHBG—who generally are less likely to do well on a TD than a shot, anyway.

So how do you actually apply the T gel? Here is what I tell my guys: Pump it onto the inside of one forearm, and then rub the forearms together. Some can get away with this, but others will need to finish off by rubbing the forearms up and down against their sides. Then always look in the mirror, as a line of T gel may be hiding on the back side of your forearms. This brings excellent absorption.

The reason you never want to use your hands to rub it in is because the surfaces of your palms are like leather; it will soak in, like hand lotion, but never make it to your bloodstream. Loss in this way is about a gram. If you are using a 1% gel, losing a gram is not so bad. But if you are using a 10% gel, for instance, a gram is a lot of T to throw away. You don't want to waste any of that good Man Gel. No wonder so many guys report "the gel did nothing for me".

If you would like to see a video we made on how to apply transdermals (it applies to all types, which would also include DHEA and pregnenolone), here it is:

http://www.youtube.com/watch?v=gXHQ7uSCxZo

While we are on this point, I'd like to point out how many times I have heard men say "the gel did nothing for me". But when I ask them what they mean, they report the gel did not raise their T levels. Digging in a little further, I ask them how many hours it was between application of the gel and the lab draw. They usually scrunch their noses, and calculate something on the order of "27 hours". As it turns out their physicians told them to skip their dose, and go in for labs. They are then being tested in a state they would not normally find themselves.

> **COMMON SENSE: *In order to measure the level of a drug in your body, you must take that drug.***

By the way, when I also ask them how they felt, many admit they did feel better. I'm betting if they had done their blood draw appropriately--a couple hours after application--they would show an appreciable increase.

...or they were simply under-dosed.

...or their estrogen rose too high, and obliterated the benefits they would otherwise have enjoyed.

Absorption is improved, especially in the dry winter months, if a good emollient is applied to the skin, about twelve hours off from the TD application. The oily skin lotion would otherwise form a barrier against absorption of the gel-base testosterone. Water and oil don't mix.

But keeping the skin nice and soft helps a lot; especially if a "T frost" forms on your skin. In that case, consider spreading the gel over a larger surface area.

And don't keep rubbing the gel. Apply it, smoothly and evenly, and let it do its job. For some reason, some guys just keep rubbing and rubbing, and they evaporate off all the alcohol that would otherwise have carried the testosterone into the skin. The testosterone powder ends up on the floor.

IF you do all this, and still aren't seeing an increase in serum T level, check thyroid function, with a Free T3.

TESTOSTERONE INJECTION

I'll start out by describing the drawbacks of injectable testosterone. They are inconvenient for patients who do not wish to give themselves their own injections, as they must then make weekly trips to their doctor's office. Why injectable test MUST be dosed at no greater than a seven day interval is because any longer than that, and you have to inject this huge dose that goes to anabolic steroid levels at first, then leaves you below where you started by the end of the second week. That puts patients on a rollercoaster which is both brutal and cruel. Guys feel the difference, across the week, even when injections are done every seven days.

Injections also expose the patient to the risks—however small—of bleeding and infection.

Taking T shots means literally hundreds of holes poked in your body over a lifetime. Some guys just hate shots; although I have noticed patients who had initially claimed this, but admitted, once they had come to enjoy the benefits of TRT, very much look forward to their shot day. And no doubt an invasive delivery system brings more risk than, for instance, a testosterone gel or cream, although I have yet to hear of a single bad outcome from any of the tens of thousands of injections my patients have self-administered.

As a good and proper Osteopathic physician, I am loath to introduce any substance to the body not absolutely necessary. Therefore, the oil, and preservative, necessary to the injectable preparation also give gels an edge.

When considering dosing of testosterone cypionate, it is important to remember that, due to the weight of the cypionate ester, a 100mg injection delivers about 70mg of testosterone. This is important to keep in mind when comparing the effects of a 100mg weekly injection of testosterone cypionate to that delivered by, for instance, T gels. With respect to absorbability—and subjective response-- you just can't compare doses between different testosterone delivery systems.

TESTOSTERONE PATCHES

These can be effective, and many find them very convenient to use. But approaching 2/3's of the patients who use them will develop a contact dermatitis *at some point*. Another drawback is some patients report they are constantly aware of their placement, and the patches are embarrassingly obvious to other gentlemen in certain public places, such as the locker room.

Speaking of "certain places", the scrotal application variety of testosterone patches are....interesting. That's all I am going to say about that, other than to note that passing testosterone through the scrotum dramatically elevates DHT, for better or worse.

TESTOSTERONE PELLETS

In my opinion, they are absolutely Stone Age. Sorry. Granted, they can work *somewhat*, and provide extra revenue for the doctor, by virtue of a billable office-based procedure. However, needlessly exposing patients to the risks ALL surgeries pose—hemorrhage and infection—is unwarranted, in my opinion, for TRT. They also can be quite painful.

Some have issues with pellet extrusion (they end up in the guy's shorts), but that risk is highly dependent upon clinician technique.

But the real issue, in my opinion, is concerned with dosing. Let's say you attempt to establish a "usual" initial dose for the pellets. There is absolutely no way to predict, up front, how a patient will react to a given dose of testosterone--regardless of the delivery system, patient's body weight, activity level or composition.

So the doctor buries these pellets in the patient's backside, and draws follow-up labs in a month or so. What are you to do if the total testosterone ends up greatly exceeding the top of normal range? And what if the pellets do not elevate T enough? Will you then go back in to implant more (and pay for the procedure)? How are you to then calculate the next dose? As tricky as dosing is for other, much more easily controlled testosterone delivery systems, I just don't see the need to add in another variable.

Worse, what if follow-up assay demonstrates markedly elevated PSA, given common current attitudes about PSA and TRT? Think about it.

Testosterone pellets do have some benefit in that selected patients may believe it more convenient to come in at longer intervals, and then be done with it for a while. If your patient is on his way to conquer Mt. Everest, or on safari, then TRT via pellet implantation is preferable to abstinence from TRT; especially at physically challenging times.

– CHAPTER EIGHT –

Human Chorionic Gonadotropin (HCG)

Even though you inject it, HCG therapy is not actually a testosterone delivery system. Instead, it causes the body to produce more testosterone on its own, in a more "natural" fashion, if you will.

Human chorionic gonadotropin (HCG) is a hormone, originally derived from the urine of pregnant women (it's what they were looking for when they "killed the rabbit" in early pregnancy testing), which mimics Luteinizing Hormone (LH) for males. Therefore it stimulates the testicles to make more testosterone (as it does the other effects of LH in the body).

It would make sense then for HCG to be used in cases of Hypogonadotropic (secondary) Hypogonadism, where the pituitary gland does not produce enough LH to adequately drive the testes into sufficient testosterone production.

The increased testosterone production induced by the HCG is still sensed by the hypothalamus and pituitary, as is all testosterone, DHT and estrogen in the bloodstream. Subsequent LH production can be reduced, if it wasn't already; thus inhibition of the HPTA is possible. Therefore

HCG does not "restart" the HPTA; other than the fact it can restore the quiescent testicles if they have been shut down, for instance, after taking anabolic steroids or prohormones. This restoration brings them to a position of being ready, willing and able to respond to any LH coming in to them through the testicular arteries.

A real benefit of HCG is that it *can* prevent testicular atrophy. I do not think we should ignore the aesthetics of that consideration. While the HCG does not really stimulate the majority of the mass of the testicle—which are the sperm-producing Sertoli cells, instead of the testosterone producing Leydig cells--many guys report their testicles did not atrophy at all on TRT if they take it. Others still do, to some degree, irrespective of HCG dosing. Everyone is different; just as some men experience no shrinkage whatsoever, even on heavy anabolic steroid cycles (when they weren't also taking HCG).

Because HCG stimulates the testes, it can have benefit with respect to maintaining fertility. Many of my patients, who are on TRT long term with regular HCG shots included, have fathered children.

By the way, HCG nasal sprays and sublingual drops have never been shown to elevate serum HCG levels. They simply don't get into the bloodstream. Their efficacy could be easily proven with a single large dose, and a urine pregnancy test. The day they spend $20, and produce a positive result, is the day I will recommend them.

Many years ago I found very low doses, (compared to the common practice of taking massive amounts of HCG—as much as 5000 IU per shot) of HCG quite sufficient. The strategy is to provide a physiologic (within normal range) serum concentration of this LH mimic. This not only makes the testicles produce what they *can*, it also makes them work *at their best*. Much is made on the message boards about potential inhibition of testosterone production by long-term HCG use. That only happens when you take too much. When you think about it, IF achieving what amounts to a normal range of a LH mimic down-regulates, then everyone would be naturally down-regulated.

But taking too much is bad for you; as with all other hormones, and medications. And taking too much HCG does not produce more testosterone, as there are only so many Leydig cells to stimulate, but does alter the pathways in ways that produce excess estrogen and progesterone—two highly feminizing hormones in men. Almost no HCG-only protocol should need estrogen control.

That is why my starting dose is only 100 IU of HCG per day, and always administered by subcutaneous injection. There is absolutely no reason to poke more holes in your muscles with longer, larger, more painful needles. Using a tiny insulin needle into the belly fat works just fine.

In following our strategy of trying to establish as normal a hormonal landscape as possible while on TRT, it makes sense to take that "physiologic" dose of HCG every day. This is just as if there were a comparable concentration of LH in the bloodstream normally. This best counters the lack of endogenous (normally produced) LH from the pituitary. Of note, there are LH receptors all over in the body, and they must be there for good reasons. I think this is why the guys who take regular doses of HCG, while on any TRT protocol, seem to do better. Those receptors—used to receiving LH stimulation that is now absent—are working again.

Looking at the hormonal pathways, LH and therefore its mimic, HCG stimulates the P450scc enzyme to convert more cholesterol into pregnenolone. This has been shown in numerous studies, and is intuitive. As men not on TRT who need more testosterone normally get an increase in LH, this pushes more of the "building blocks" of the hormones downstream to make them, since they are all made from the cholesterol molecular framework (the word "steroids" comes from: choleSTERol). A hormone known as ACTH does the same thing, to produce more adrenal hormones.

So you can see that HCG not only stimulates the testicles to produce more testosterone, it first produces more of the raw materials needed to make the testosterone molecule as well. The wisdom of the body is infinite.

As previously stated, I like to start out giving no more than 100 IU of HCG per day, as a *starting* dose. And please give it some time to work; about three weeks. It takes a while for the LH receptors to adjust. Increase by no more than 50 IU per day, now with just a few days at each addition, to see if you feel anything. When you "start low and go slow" (a strategy applied to all proper hormonal supplementation), not only do you know what direction to go from the initial dose, if it doesn't work, you have not overshot your mark. Taking a double dose every other day seems to work better in some guys (as long as you don't go over 500 IU per shot). You will have to experiment; every-body is different.

Taking HCG at night produces a more normal spike of testosterone production while you sleep. But taking it in the morning provides an increased sense of well-being, and libido, during the day. So many patients have told me this, it makes me appreciate the benefits of stimulating the LH receptors found elsewhere in the body—they must be there for good reasons — such as in the more peripheral (emotional) centers of the brain. The effects are too soon after taking the HCG shot to come from induced testosterone production.

HCG breaks down at room temperature. So get the vials good and cold before you reconstitute it, and keep it in the bottom (coldest) part of the refrigerator.

I have now seen evidence reconstituted HCG can be refrozen.

HCG AND TESTOSTERONE SHOTS

For those on injectable testosterone, there are several good options, depending upon how you take your shots. The daily HCG injection is always good, and most physiologic. But you have to then appreciate it will add to the peak in serum testosterone levels produced by the testosterone shot.

If you take a weekly testosterone injection, you can add in a higher dose of HCG (starting at 250 IU, and working up to as much as 500 IU per shot) on the last two days of the injection week, Day Six and Day Seven, with the testosterone cypionate injection day being Day One. For instance, if you inject your testosterone cypionate on Fridays, take your HCG on Wednesday and Thursday. This not only can keep the testicles up to size, it also produces more testosterone naturally, so counters the drop in serum testosterone level, by the end of the week, brought by the half-life of the cypionate ester on the testosterone cypionate molecule. Granted, taking a little HCG every day will cause the spike in serum T go even higher, superimposed on top of that produced by the T injection.

Taking HCG on the last two days of the injection week has been come to be known as "The Crisler Method". This name was first used by Dr. Ronald Rothenberg, whom I consider the finest Anti-Aging Medicine physician in the country, and a really good fellow, back in 2005.

When doing your follow-up laboratory testing, do not take the HCG under this protocol. That means, for instance, if you take your testosterone cypionate shot on Friday, and want to do your labs on Thursday to see where you are at the lowest point of the week, do not take your HCG on Wednesday. Instead, have your labs drawn on Thursday, then take your HCG shot afterward. That way you can best titrate (adjust to best effect) the dose of the testosterone shot, without the HCG clouding the picture.

If my patients take their HCG every day, or every other day, then I do have them stay on schedule with it for their labs. This is because the HCG is always then at play, and I test my patients "where they live'.

And, as always, NEVER do labs on a testosterone injection day. That means—by the previous example—not having them drawn Friday morning, then take your shot. You are then testing on Day Eight, by my system, which is a state you are never in; only do testing "where you live". Sometimes patients do this in order to try to get more testosterone. The date of the blood collection is right on the laboratory printout.

Once is a great while a patient will tell me, when I point out the date of the blood collection, that he actually took his shot a couple days earlier (for *whatever* reason). He then finds out, unfortunately, in doing so he invalidated his labs.

Many, especially those with lower SHBG levels, do better by splitting their testosterone shot each week. Taking half the dose, twice each week, actually produces an increase in total dose (please see the section on subcutaneous injections), by effect. It is important here to pick the same two days each week; in other words, it is not the same as taking a shot every three days. This improves compliance, and helps with dosing. I prefer Tuesdays and Fridays (especially with the new subcutaneous shot protocol). Given, this amounts to a three day—four day—three day interval. But such a regimen provides a bit more for the weekend. The extra, fourth day, then falls on Monday....and who cares about Mondays, anyway?

With the split, twice weekly testosterone dosing regimen—which produces very stable levels throughout the week, so we pretty much just accept the numbers on the labs as consistent—daily HCG shots are just great; and provide even more entropy (randomness) in the serum androgen profile across the day. Or, you can take a larger shot on each of the days just prior to the two testosterone shot days; starting with 250 IU of HCG per shot, and going as high as 500 IU per shot; a modification of The Crisler Method.

HCG AND TRANSDERMAL TESTOSTERONE DELIVERY SYSTEMS

With a daily T gel (the only way to take it), a daily HCG shot to go along with it is wonderful. In fact, in my professional opinion, this is the very best TRT regimen out there. Combined with "backfilling" the pathways (please see that section), such a regimen most closely approximates the hormonal milieu of a young, healthy man. And *that* is the ultimate goal of TRT medicine.

But you could still take your HCG twice per week, or every other day, whatever works best for your particular lifestyle, and level of commitment.

I have provided a paper detailing some of HCG's amazing benefits for TRT medicine at:

www.allthingsmale.com/publications.html.

MIXING AND STORING HCG

Store your HCG in the box it came in, to keep it in the dark, and in the refrigerator or freezer.

Make sure to cool the vial of bacteriostatic water first, so it will already be cold when you reconstitute it.

I exclusively like a 10:1 ratio of units of HCG to bacteriostatic water. I do not like stronger concentrations. That means, for instance, a 10,000iu vial is reconstituted with 10mL of bac water. If the vial contains 5000iu of lyophylized (dried) HCG powder, then add 5mL of bac water. This way, you can conveniently use insulin syringes for subcutaneous injections (no reason to do intramuscular); 10 units on an insulin syringe provides 100iu of HCG.

Draw the bac water from the vial, and keep the vial containing the HCG powder upright as you inject the solution. Withdraw the same amount of air from the vial as fluid injected. Doing so will prevent the reconstituted HCG from spraying back out the small hole when you pull the needle out of the rubber septum.

– CHAPTER NINE –

SELECTIVE ESTROGEN RECEPTOR MODULATORS (SERM)

This class of drugs was first developed to treat women's health issues. As were the aromatase inhibitors (AIs). But we use AI's to actually lower the production of estrogen; while SERM's are used to just block estrogen that has already been made. Both classes of drugs have found useful purposes in our field of medicine—and are prescribed more now for men than the gender for whom they were originally developed.

The two most popular medications in use from this class are Clomid (clomiphene) and Nolvadex (tamoxifen).

SERMs can increase testosterone production, by fooling the pituitary gland into producing more Luteinizing Hormone

(LH), which then goes into the blood stream, and stimulates the testicles. The hypothalamus and pituitary constantly monitor estrogen levels, and if it *appears* low (because the estrogen receptors found there have been blocked by the SERM), they increase the drive to make more testosterone. Estrogen levels naturally drop when testosterone production falls; because estrogen is made from testosterone. So LH goes up, to increase testosterone.

This class of drugs have been used for many years in fertility medicine; administered to both men and women. They can improve fertility because they elevate LH and FSH levels in both sexes; this is why they are good for increasing testosterone, and simultaneously, testicular size, in men.

But a very real problem with this class of drugs is they are at once estrogen antagonists (receptor blockers) and agonists (actually act as an estrogen). About half of what is in that clomiphene pill blocks estrogen (enclomiphene), and the other half *is* an estrogen (zuclomiphene). So when you are blocking estrogen at some receptors, you are simultaneously adding an estrogen that binds to the estrogen receptors, and stimulates, others. That is why this class of drugs has the name it does.

The conventional dosing for Clomid (clomiphene) had been, for many years, 50mg per day; and roughly half of that is an estrogen (female hormone). This is an important point.

Because of the estrogen-like half of the drug, SERMs *can* make SHBG levels soar (estrogens can do that), in *some* men. I do hope it does not spread across the message boards that no one should take them, as if this happens to everyone.

Therefore they may have a great increase in testosterone (when it works effectively) but experience no benefit, as the free testosterone goes down because of increased SHBG. As a result they may even feel worse than when they started. You just have to try, run labs, see how you feel, and find out. But the benefit of being able to simply drop a pill every day, as the sum total of your TRT regimen, certainly has value. This protocol is also quite inexpensive.

Of note, in some cases adding an aromatase inhibitor (AI) to a Clomid-only protocol improves things. You could even have them compounded into the same capsule.

My friend Dr. Eugene Shippen, author of the bestselling book "The Testosterone Syndrome" first came to realize the usual dose of Clomid is too high, because of the estrogen load it presents. Many years ago we had lunch, at a medical conference in Orlando, where we sat down together and compared notes. We both had found half that dose effective. He has since gone on to report just a quarter tablet, 12.5mgs, per day—or even every other day—works for many. Remember the adage: "start low and go slow".

Hence, I usually start patients who suffer Hypothalamic (secondary) Hypogonadism, and want to try a SERM-only therapy, at 12.5mgs per day of clomiphene. I run labs 3 weeks later, and always include a LH and FSH, since we are looking to induce increases in them with the clomiphene. Depending on what those labs say, I may then increase to 25mg, then 37.5mgs QD, with follow-up labs—and comparison to subjective response--at each step. Rarely do I go to 50mg QD. It all depends on what we see, with respect to levels of LH and FSH.

I have found if a patient is suffering ill effects of estrogenic symptoms with a given dose of SERM, there usually is no point in increasing that dose further.

It's important to tell the patient that how he feels with the addition of *any* TRT protocol may have nothing to do with his resultant level of testosterone. That might sound strange, but until you run the labs, there is no way to tell what the effect actually has been. In any TRT protocol, elevated estrogen can kill positive subjective response. And as we just explored, Clomiphene (due to its half estrogen-like nature) can elevate SHBG, and you end up right back where you started with respect to Free T levels. Since you have now seized control of the HPTA with the TRT, normal feedback mechanisms are no longer in play.

Or perhaps it's just that the estrogen half of the SERM can really bother a guy, and so the benefit of the increased testosterone is greatly dampened. The overall strategy is to block estrogen at the hypothalamus and pituitary sufficiently, without simultaneously adding in more estrogen mimic than his body can handle. You just have to try and see.

– CHAPTER TEN –

Treating Gynecomastia

Another SERM class drug, Nolvadex (tamoxifen), I prefer for preventing gynecomastia ("Man Boobs") when my patients have "nipple issues". First, of course, is to directly address the real problem, where possible, which may just be elevated estrogen. Just a change in the strategy of TRT regimen, or even the addition of an aromatase inhibitor, is first.

But some guys come in with just gynecomastia, or have intermittent problems, from some as yet unidentified cause. For them, I start with 20mg of Nolvadex, twice per day, for a couple weeks, until the symptoms disappear. Then 30mg per day, then 20mg per day, 10mg per day; all for one to two week intervals. And done. The taper is important.

IF you can catch the gyno within the first few months, you can usually get rid of it. Beyond that, consider surgical options.

– CHAPTER ELEVEN –

Aromatase Inhibitors (AI)

Aromatase (AKA "estrogen synthetase") is the name of the enzyme that converts testosterone into estrogen. This class of drugs interferes with the actions of aromatase, and was created to treat breast cancer in women. Now way more men are on them than women.

There are two types of AI's (1) the so-called "suicide inhibitors" — which should actually be called aromatase *inactivators*--such as Aromasin (exemestane), and (2) the "competitive inhibitors" — which have to compete in the area around the aromatase enzyme with estrogen--like Arimidex (anastrazole), and Femara (letrozole) — for binding to the aromatase enzyme.

A risk of using an AI *improperly* is one of driving estrogen levels too low, with deleterious consequences for the lipid profile, bone density, endothelial function, libido, etc. The joints can also dry out, and hurt, and you can get headaches (a common complaint on the message boards). So be careful to not take too much; and "too much" is highly individualized. Since the aromatase enzyme lives in higher concentrations in fat, obese men are more likely to need them. Conversely, once he loses twenty pounds, his estrogen levels may drop sufficiently; so that a guy who previously needed an AI, now no longer does. If he stays on it (or at a previous, higher dose) he could end up driving his estrogen too low. This is another reason why I run labs on my guys every six months—a lot can happen in that amount of time.

As with all drugs, there are people who are just sensitive to a given drug or class of drugs. Some men may need to switch to another medication within this group to achieve the desired effects.

I generally prefer to work with Arimidex (anastrazole). It just seems gentler. I am well familiar with it, so it is the one I will describe here in detail. It is now readily available, and quite inexpensive, in generic form.

The dosing of meds of this class is highly variable. And please keep in mind it takes a while for the medication to work its way deep into the tissues, as Dr. Shippen has pointed out, so give the introduction, or change in dosing, a month before drawing labs, and assessing how it makes you feel (it takes that long for SHBG to stabilize, anyway; remember its effects on free hormone levels). Subjective response can change across the weeks, as it seems to be with all medications used in this field of medicine.

If estrogen is a problem only right after you take your testosterone shot, then take it at the same time. As testosterone rises from the shot—and so conversion to estrogen—it will be there to block the aromatase enzyme. This works for some, whether they take one, two, or three testosterone shots per week. Start out with 0.25mg at a time. You may need to take 0.5mg with each shot. Any more than that, add extra doses throughout the week.

Those on TD's need more regular dosing, of course, because of the daily multiple spikes in testosterone. Usually start with

0.25mg QOD (every other day). If you need more, take 0.5mg QOD (easier to cut them in half than into quarters). Some may need to take some every day, even as much as 0.5mg QD (every day).

I have seen very rare cases where the gentleman required 1mg per day, and even one patient who required 2mg per day, of Arimidex.

It's okay to just bite them in half. Sit the other half somewhere safe, and take it the next time. That way if you eat a little too much one time, it evens out with the next dose.

Don't try to save time by cutting up a bunch of them all at once. The smaller pieces float to the top of the bottle, and you end up increasing your dose as you get toward the bottom. Powder falls off, as well, and is wasted.

Compounding pharmacies will make troches containing aromatase inhibitors in them. It seems to take less medication when you put it under your tongue, so it must be getting in. Or you can just put the tablet under your tongue, and save the cost of manufacturing the troche (although considerations for the changing pH within the oral cavity can bring added benefits for well-made troches). Anastrazole doesn't taste bad at all. It takes a good compounder to make troches well, and they are somewhat expensive. But some guys only need 0.1mg of anastrazole at a time like this; that is impossible to provide by cutting up tiny little 1mg tablets.

Only in very rare cases have I used an Aromatase Inhibitor (AI) as sole therapy. As with blocking estrogen at the hypothalamus and pituitary increases LH production (and therefore testosterone), actually lowering estrogen does the same. But doing so—in sufficient dosing to create a good testosterone increase—usually lowers estrogens to unhealthy levels. But there are individuals, although very few of them, who benefit by simply inhibiting this conversion.

Anastrazole is now generic. This lowered the cost tremendously, and brought proper TRT administration within reach of many more men.

– CHAPTER TWELVE –

Drugs Used For Performance Enhancement

Finally, in my professional opinion, Deca-Durabolin (nandrolone), or Winstrol (stanozolol) have no place in TRT medicine. There is no such thing as a "Deca deficiency".

Deca has a nasty side effect profile, including uncontrollable progesterone-like effects (including gynecomastia), HPTA suppression, and substantial risk of long-term impotence. And there is no medical indication for the attainment of large amounts of muscle mass, other than in documented cases of wasting disease.

I would like to add the prediction that long-term use of Deca will one day prove to increase the risk of serious health issues. It is a drug of the class called progestins – synthetic progesterone. Progestins have been shown to increase the risk of cardiovascular events, and even cancer, in women. And as it would appear what is bad for the breast is similarly bad for the prostate....

Finally, use of the word "steroid" should be avoided in our field. The hill is steep enough already.

– CHAPTER THIRTEEN –

The Meat And Potatoes of TRT

Now we will delve into the general strategy for administering TRT.

The decision is made, by the doctor *together* with the patient (and you are now well equipped to participate), as to which of the various testosterone delivery systems you are going to try first. Be prepared to make adjustments, and try other application methods if necessary. And PLEASE don't let "some guy" on an Internet message board try to push you one way or the other—there is a LOT of bad info out there. And, as I always say, every-body is different.

You just don't know which modality will be best for you, until you try. You may have a built-in personal preference, due to an absolute unwillingness to self-inject, risk of accidental transfer to a female partner who may be/become pregnant, a baby in the house (better hug them while you can—after they hit 13 you won't get within arm's reach) lifestyle which does not allow for use of a transdermal gel, etc. But for a given application, every-body reacts differently to hormonal manipulation. Some hyper-respond to a given initial dose, others show hardly any bump in serum T levels on same. Yet when you switch to a different delivery system, on initial dosing, they may convert to very high androgen levels.

The same is true of the subjective benefits from TRT. I have patients who love testosterone gel because it successfully treated their Erectile Dysfunction (the expected outcome because of increased DHT production), others get more from testosterone shots. My experience thus far has taught me two lessons:

(1) You don't know how you will react to a given dose/system until you try and (2) nothing surprises me anymore.

The question of which testosterone delivery system to try first (SERM, HCG-only, TD, shots) is one which brings much confusion amongst beginning practitioners of TRT. I would, when possible, always start out a patient on a testosterone gel (once other options for increasing testosterone more naturally have failed, and a pure T delivery system is so required). Ease of application, avoidance of physical intrusion by injection, and increased probability of successful sexual dysfunction treatment make this so. Also, stable serum levels are attained quickly, determination of successful treatment is more forthcoming (although the manufacturer of these products recommends at least a couple months as adequate trial of therapy). If the labs AND patient's answers to follow-up subjective questioning lead to a switch to testosterone shots, the conversion is an easy one to make. Simply D/C (discontinue) the gel, give the shot, and carry on.

However, if a patient is started out on shots, it's more difficult, and complicated, to switch back to a gel, as a sequential taper must be initiated. Care should be taken to not overindulge serum androgen levels. Anabolic steroid-like serum levels may "spoil" the TRT patient, and subsequent subjective expectations needlessly inflated.

Of note, the heightened subjective benefits of high testosterone levels fall away over time; even reverse.

And there is nothing wrong, for those with hypothalamic hypogonadism, with trying a SERM-class drug first, or HCG-only. Many men do wonderfully on either, even both these TRT modalities. I've combined them, in the same patient.

There simply is no way to predict how a particular patient will respond—not Medical History (i.e. number, or severity, of symptoms), body weight, baseline hormone levels, even anabolic steroid history (although they, for some unknown reason, often need more to make them feel right). I have had very slight gentlemen barely elevate on 100mg of testosterone cypionate per week, and massively muscled former steroid athletes who went over the top of "normal" range on the same dosage (with similar baselines). Likewise, one man may see only a modest increase in DHT on the starting dose of Androgel/Testim/Fortesta/Axiron, another may become quite supraphysiologic on same.

In most cases, I start my guys out on T gel at 50mg QD or testosterone cypionate 80mg per week. The test cypionate must be administered in weekly injections, as opposed to taking twice the dosage every other week. Some physicians STILL dose every third or fourth week, producing wide swings in serum androgen levels. Where else in medicine does a physician dose a medication completely void of any consideration for the half-life of the drug? This puts the patient on a physical, and emotional, roller coaster, as they are at anabolic steroid levels right off the bat, but then below baseline by the end of the second week. It also increases the risk of developing polycythemia, greatly accentuates aromatase activity (therefore unnecessarily elevating estrogen production, perhaps then requiring aromatase inhibition), and takes a more massive volume of IM injection into the muscle tissue.

The last point is thought, by the sheer volume of the new long-acting Aveed testosterone injectable, to increase the risk of immediate cardiovascular event. This is why patients on that drug must remain at the physician's office for half an hour after the injection. I will have more to say about Aveed in future publishings.

In order to get the serum androgen concentration to a stable level more quickly, I sometimes "frontload" (double dose) the first injection. This shortens the 2.5 half-life requirement Pharmacology teaches us it takes to attain stable serum levels of a drug.

No other medications which manipulate hormone levels are provided (except for HCG), until follow-up labs are returned (i.e. aromatase inhibition). I have seen estrogen drop on its own, after initiating TRT. Additionally, you want to be able to find out just how that given dose of testosterone affects the entire system, on its own. This opportunity is missed otherwise.

For test cypionate patients, the second panel is run following the fourth or fifth injection. I also keep in mind the coordination of the injection with the lab draw, as peak serum levels are attained at about the 48 hour point, then fall as the week goes on. I always want the labs drawn the second half of the injection week, after things have stabilized more.

Transdermals can be rechecked in as early as two weeks, but a full month provides complete stabilization, especially of SHBG. TD's stabilize Total Testosterone level, for most, by the end of the second or third day.

Dosing changes are made, once follow-up lab work is back, and the patient is interviewed regarding their subjective reports of changes in libido, sexual performance, fatigue, strength, mental outlook, etc. I do not allow them to see their lab work prior to their interview, as doing so may artificially influence their subjective report. Men are finicky, and will match their subjective response to what they *think* they are seeing with their numbers.

Often they will tell you they felt "incredible" the first couple of weeks (and bursting with libido), but they don't feel quite as good now. This is because subjective findings are the best while serum androgen levels are accelerating. Adjunctive to this phenomenon is the fact their HPTA was not yet suppressed, so their endogenous production was higher than it would be by the end of the month, and there is a burst of dopamine playing to upregulated dopamine receptors in the first days as well. TRT patients are always HPTA-suppressed to greater or lesser degree. And Bioavailable Estrogen may not have risen yet, so same is not masking the benefits of the testosterone supplementation.

Much weight is placed upon the patient's subjective findings, as they are not likely to remain compliant in the TRT program unless they feel noticeably better, irrespective of the much less obvious long term improvements in health. Certainly, if the patient reports they are quite happy at a Total Testosterone level of 600ng/dl, you should not increase the dosage. As a practical limit, the top of "normal" range for Total Testosterone provides a ceiling, more or less, above which we can expect to find the benefits of TRT beginning to reverse. I have had many patients find a return of their libido when they went from twice normal range down into the upper quartile, once I took over their care.

If SHBG level is high, you may need to go a bit over the top of range in order to produce satisfactory Bioavailable T. This is another reason you need your TRT managed by someone who really knows what they are doing. There REALLY is a difference!

Changes in shot dosing are made in small increments, as response to same is not linear. That includes the conversion to estrogen as well. It is convenient and practical to increase, or decrease shot dosing (for those on once weekly shots) by 10 or 20mg at a time, per week—no more. But how much actual testosterone is being added?

The actual testosterone molecule makes up only 70% of the weight of the testosterone cypionate. The rest is the weight of the ester. So 100mg of testosterone cypionate is really 70mg of testosterone. Normal males produce from 5-15 mg of testosterone naturally. So when you add 20mg of testosterone cypionate, which is—at the 200mg/ml concentration—14mg of additional testosterone per week. An average of 2mg per day. This is why an increase of only one tick mark on the syringe produces a significant increase in testosterone dosing. "Start low—go SLOW".

As previously mentioned, how the TRT patient feels is largely dependent upon which *direction* his serum androgen levels are moving. If a guy is at 1000ng/dl, for instance, and he is lowered down to 800ng/dl, he may really feel it. But he is still at 800ng/dl! In time, however, things even back out. And the reverse is also true. By the way, this is why testosterone troches are sometimes of great benefit, as they quickly accelerate serum androgen levels (we will explore the limited use of sublingual testosterone preparations in a future release).

For the Big Pharma produced T gel patients, we are more limited by their provided mechanisms, with respect to dosing changes. They are all good, but no doubt more flexibility is provided through compounded products, for those committed to the employment of transdermal testosterone delivery systems.

Never just start out on an aromatase inhibitor. Clinics that do are there for the purpose of selling drugs. The need for estrogen control must be proven first. We would have otherwise added an unnecessary medication. Should the patient develop any "nipple issues" secondary to accelerating serum androgen levels and/or elevated estrogen, you cannot start them on a SERM right away (unless that is the TRT modality you are employing, of course) because doing so will invalidate your evaluation at follow-up. Of note, males can experience these "nipple issues" even while estrogen levels are within physiological range, due to mere changes in hormone levels—like during puberty. But know this: you will not grow breasts in one month.

– CHAPTER FOURTEEN –

Subcutaneous Testosterone Injections

I favor this topic so much, it got its own chapter.

The legendary Dr. Eugene Shippen (author of the New York Times Best Seller "The Testosterone Syndrome" as well as the Foreword to this book) first introduced me to subcutaneous injection testosterone administration. He told me he learned about it from South African physician Neil Burman, but now has been actively exploring its possibilities for at least fifteen years.

At first the concept seemed kind of strange; as I am sure it does to you. Especially after remembering what happened when I made the mistake of throwing empty automobile oil cans into a plastic garbage bag as a teen; my father was not happy with my learning experience about mixing oil-based substances (no amount of scrubbing removed the stain from the garage floor, after they melted through). So injecting the oil directly into fat, and risking either dissolving tissue or some other unknown, untoward long-term response, left me happy to let other doctors' patients serve as the guinea pigs. Additionally, the higher concentration of aromatase produced in adipose (fat) tissue predictably could unnecessarily increase the injected testosterone's conversion to estrogen.

A more amusing experience, from more recent memory, was walking into the auditorium at a medical conference, nearly a decade ago. Dr. Shippen was on stage, with hundreds of physician attendees in the audience, hanging on his every word. The screen overhead showed a slide of teaching points about subcutaneous testosterone injection technique. Without breaking rhythm Dr. Shippen quipped into the microphone "I wonder when Dr. Crisler will get with it and try this".

Now I have, professionally and personally. And we are glad we did!

Please let me calm your hesitation by divulging that not only are hundreds of my patients delighted with their results, many of the top doctors in our field now are promoting it heavily. Subcutaneous (SC) injections are truly at the cutting edge of medicine, as many men who have tried them now greatly prefer same over their previous intramuscular (IM) method.

To be clear, we should think of this technique as injecting into the fat, not just under the skin. If you are interested in less painful shots, no holes in your muscles, no bruising, and making your bottle of testosterone cypionate last longer, this may be something for you to consider. And most of my patients tell me their libido improves as well. Surely, it is much better for those who must inject more than once per week.

As you have no doubt noticed, I'm not much for posting the results of scientific studies. But for those who are not influenced by the subjective reports of thousands of men from around the world, several studies have been reported which demonstrate several benefits of this new (actually, not so new) method of administering TRT.

The first one I will present involved both classical hypogonadal males and female-to-male transsexuals. Notice they achieved very good serum testosterone levels— using relatively low doses, practically "TRT Light" (50-60mg per week)--and there were no adverse reactions among the 20 tested individuals. They also found lower Doses, taken SC, just as effective as a somewhat higher dose which was previously injected IM. "SC T was well tolerated and produced therapeutic serum concentrations at doses generally lower than required for IM injections."

This is an important point, because, to an Osteopathic physician, fewer drugs are always better. Here it is:

Evaluation of the efficacy of subcutaneous administration of testosterone in female to male transexuals and hypogonadal males.
Savage, MD, Alan Howard Morris, MD, Michael A Dedekian, MD1 and Daniel I Spratt, MD. Endocr Rev, Vol. 34 (03_MeetingAbstracts): MON-594 Copyright © 2013 by The Endocrine Society

There is another, from 2006—so it has been studied for some time. Again, no bad reactions. "This is the first report, which demonstrated the efficacy of delivering weekly testosterone using this cheap, safe, and less painful subcutaneous route. "

Subcutaneous administration of testosterone. A pilot study report.
Al-Futaisi AM, Al-Zakwani IS, Almahrezi AM, Morris D. Saudi Med J. 2006 Dec; 27(12):1843-6.

TESTOSTERONE REPLACEMENT THERAPY

A third study concluded: "A once-week SC injection of 50-100 mg of TE appears to achieve sustainable and stable levels of physiological T. This technique offers fewer physician visits and the use of smaller quantity of medication, thus lower costs. "

STABLE TESTOSTERONE LEVELS ACHIEVED WITH SUBCUTANEOUS TESTOSTERONE INJECTIONS.

M.B. Greenspan, C.M. Chang Division of Urology, Department of Surgery, McMaster University, Hamilton, ON, Canada

IF you want to try to talk your local doctor into trying SC injections, you may want to print out these studies, and show them to him/her.

A major pharmaceutical company, called Antares, is now about to bring to market a subcutaneous testosterone autoinjector. This brings great legitimacy to this mode of TRT administration.

If you would like to see a video we made of how to inject subcutaneously, click on the link below. You'll just have to bear with the guy doing the demonstration:

http://youtu.be/n98LOFQwUGA.

Since the production of that video, I have moved my preferred injection site to the fat pad on the top of each gluteal muscle. It is as if you were doing the regular IM injection in your backside, but now using a short needle, so the injection is made into the fat. I find this to be easier, more comfortable, and less likely to cause any swelling (important for those carrying less body fat). Also, the oil does not extrude back out again. You rarely even get a single drop of blood.

I have found that 40mg of testosterone cypionate twice per week, subcutaneously, is equal to 100mg per week, IM. One of the above studies showed guys get by on less with this method, too. The reason gets a little technical, but, basically, you are clipping off the peak, and the low point, caused by a once per week IM shot. That means not only do you feel better, your bottle of testosterone cypionate lasts longer.

I have found SC especially effective for those with lower SHBG levels. These patients lose a lot of testosterone into their urine while their blood levels are rapidly rising, and so lost. That does not happen with the slower, more even release into the system produced by injecting into the fat.

Needle size is one of personal choice. Some like 25ga. at 3/8", all the way to 29ga. (yes--you can fill them), ½" insulin syringes. You will just have to experiment for yourself. But please consider using a one piece "rig", otherwise you are wasting a couple drops of precious Man Oil each time you inject, lost when you change the needle. That really adds up, across the life of the bottle, particularly if you need more than one shot per week.

– CHAPTER FIFTEEN –

"Backfilling" The Pathways

…a phrase I created.

A man who suffers Hypothalamic Hypogonadism already is deficient in the LH hormone that not only stimulates testosterone production, but also has effects elsewhere in the body.

And if a patient who has Primary Hypogonadism (testicular failure), is started on TRT, the subsequent inhibition of his HPTA induces Hypothalamic (secondary) Hypogonadism. This alters hormone levels, and their pathways, everywhere in the body. We will probably never know all the intermediary steps in these pathways, much less the heretofore untold actions of each substance upon the body.

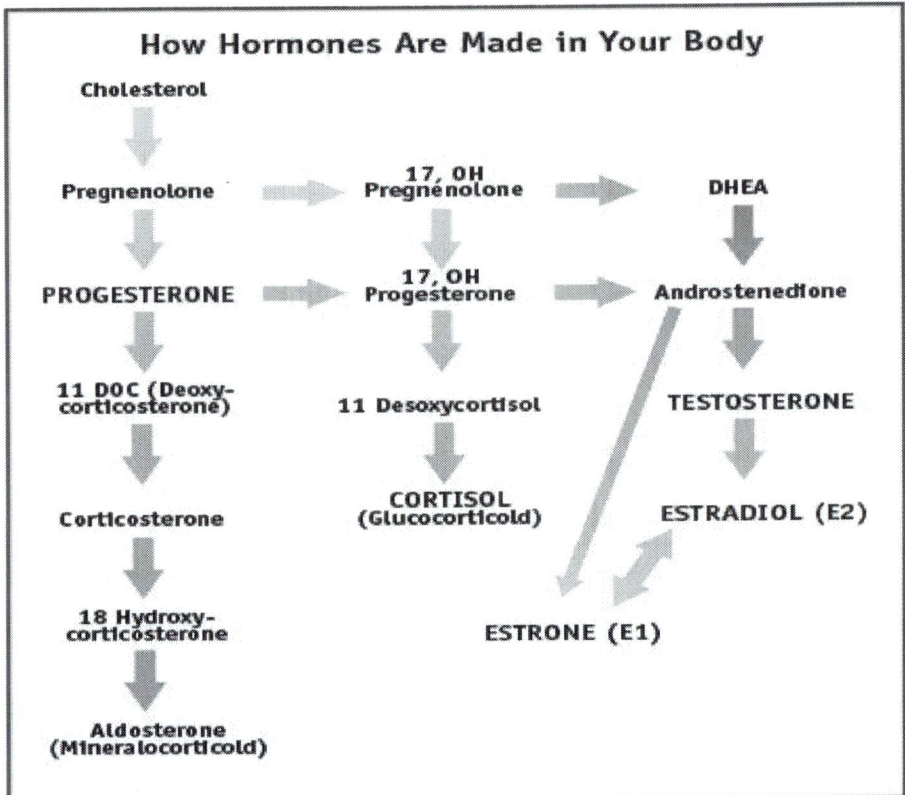

How Hormones Are Made in Your Body

Please refer back to the above diagram, and you can see why I nearly always add HCG (which stimulates conversion of cholesterol to pregnenolone), pregnenolone, and DHEA to the TRT regimen. Inserting these hormones helps restore natural hormonal pathways; "backfilling" them, if you will. This, to some extent, assists the natural production line of hormones, including the other hormones which are made from cholesterol.

I believe those who implement this strategy tend to feel better. That is what my patients tell me.

– CHAPTER SIXTEEN –

A Few Words About Laboratory Analysis and TRT

The astute practitioner must keep in mind proper assay evaluation when using a transdermal BID (twice per day) regimen. Serum T levels will appear artificially low then because only half the total daily dose is being measured. The second application of T gel is really not being measured, as it has largely dissipated from the day before. Again, the 24 hour urine panel is freed of this limitation, since it collects a fairly reliable proportion of all the T gel that found its way into the bloodstream.

I actually prefer blood testing when following injectable TRT. The 24 hour urine panel will show results which are artificially elevated if the collection is done while serum androgen levels are rapidly rising, such as right after a shot. That is because a higher percentage is being excreted into the urine during that time.

Always remember the curve of serum levels across the week with testosterone shots. Count the days after the shot, and consider what is happening then with respect to both the testosterone, and estrogen, levels. Think about any HCG that was taken. Factor in what estrogen control may have been in play. You have to keep things real.

I like to run follow-up labs every six months. It is important to monitor the general health and well-being of the patient, but also insure compliance with treatment protocols, as well as their continued effectiveness. Those who have developed Polycythemia ("thick blood") must be monitored twice per year, maybe more often; this is also an opportunity to make sure they are keeping up with their blood donations.

– CHAPTER SEVENTEEN –

Things to Look Out For

CO-MORBIDITIES

Only breast and active prostate cancer are absolute contraindications (reasons to not treat) for TRT, at this time. Patients with serious cardiac, hepatic or renal disease must be monitored carefully; this is true for all medical therapies, of course.

Also, TRT may potentiate sleep apnea in some patients. I have also found that some will actually experience an amelioration of their sleep apnea symptoms.

DRUG INTERACTIONS

TRT decreases insulin, or and/or oral diabetic medication requirements, in diabetic patients. Therefore make sure to closely monitor your blood sugar after initiating TRT, if you have diabetes.

It also increases clearance (removal from the body via the kidneys, into the urine) of propranolol (a blood pressure medication known as a beta blocker), so the dosage may need to be increased. And it decreases the clearance of oxyphenbutazone, an inflammatory drug of the NSAID class.

On a side note, the word "oxyphenbutazone" yielded the single highest possible score, 1,780 points, on a single word, ever played in the game of Scrabble.

BLOOD CLOTTING CHANGES

Potential changes in the time it takes for the blood to coagulate (clot) often scares Surgeons who are naïve about this type of medical therapy. On this topic, I am absolutely amazed when Surgeons, Anesthesiologists, Cardiologists, etc. withhold TRT prior to surgical procedures. Let's take inventory of the results of their actions: oxygen carrying capacity of the blood goes down, anabolism (tissue growth) turns to catabolism (tissue breakdown), inflammation increases, weakness and fatigue, estrogen goes through the roof, water retention, depression, etc. as the body is generally thrown into a state of turmoil. Just what you want while undergoing the physical and emotional challenges of surgery, or right after having a heart attack!

Sadly, cases where specialists actually consult with the qualified administering physician are all too rare. Another observation which is unique to TRT medicine.

Currently, much is being made about the potential for increased risk of heart attacks and strokes from TRT. So much evidence is being presented to the contrary, I will not take the space to repeat it all here. Simply, as long as the H/H is monitored, and you do not have a blood coagulability disorder, there is little to be concerned about.

– CHAPTER EIGHTEEN –

The Future of Testosterone Replacement Therapy

"The ultimate goal of TRT medicine is to optimize health and happiness in our patients. This means producing an environment where we have elevated testosterone to sufficient levels, with the body responding as if unaware of the exogenous manipulations."

— John Crisler, DO

"I've got some good news for you."

"Jack" is a 42 year old office manager who made an appointment with his doctor to finally discuss his "romantic problems". During the talk in the exam room he described how his marriage is suffering because he has lost most of his interest in sex, and has poor erectile quality anyway. He also shared how he just feels "weak all the time", and "it's hard to work because I have brain fog". He said he was having a hard time keeping up with the younger guys at work. Finally, he admitted, "all this is kind of making me feel depressed".

Jack's doctor ordered laboratory tests for his testosterone level. Three weeks later, Jack returned for his follow-up.

Immediately upon entering the room, the doctor happily announces "I've got good news for you". Then, "It's not your testosterone."

The doctor then writes prescriptions for Viagra, and an antidepressant. Once he has paid for his office visit, Jack is sent on his way.

As it turns out, Jack had been doing some poking around on the Internet, and joined a couple men's health forums (**www.AllThingsMale.com/forum** and **www.ExcelMale.com**). So when Jack's doctor told him--even though his testosterone came back at 345, in a range from 300-1000--his "testosterone is normal", Jack knew better. Jack's next call went to a doctor who specifically works with Testosterone Replacement Therapy. The two hour drive, he found out, was well worth it.

A few weeks later, Jack is now on a T gel, and a small amount of a medication that controls estrogen. His energy, and attitude, are both up. He is able to think more clearly at work, and is no longer pooped out by 3PM.

And, oh, Momma's happy again. And, as they say, IF Momma's happy.....

Made in the USA
Lexington, KY
13 August 2015